Wayside's little Post Office. *Painting by Jean Kurtis Schodorf*

During the time of Laura Ingalls Wilder and her family, everything was real — nothing was "plastic" — love permeated the air. And so it was, even with Ma Ingalls — everything she did came from her heart — from helping Pa in the field to cooking for her family.

Today, if we could discard the "plastic" and whet our appetites with the true flavor of love, understanding and kindness, what a blessing it would be.

Wilma Kurtis and Anita Gold have embodied that feeling in *Prairie Recipes and Kitchen Antiques.* It is a cookbook which every mother and daughter should enjoy together.

May I wish each and everyone a cornucopia of good wishes and a hearty appetite always.

Michael Landon

Wayside's little Post Office is no longer in operation. For future information relating to the Little House and the Ingalls family write to:

Little House On The Prairie Site
P.O. Box 110
Independence, Kansas 67301

Prairie Recipes and Kitchen Antiques

by Wilma Kurtis and Anita Gold

Published By

Wallace-Homestead Book Co.
1912 Grand
Des Moines, Iowa 50305

4

To all the good prairie people who so kindly contributed the cherished recipes that fill this book.

This replica of the Little House was built by civic group volunteers of Independence, Kansas where the original once stood in Wayside.

Special thanks to Bill Kurtis, Sr. and Cy Gold who encouraged their "favorite dishes" to "write it all down" and share with you their love of the prairie.

The early day settlers of Kansas, the word believed to mean "land of the south wind," possessed no great wealth, but they lived a rugged, and self reliant life and must have enjoyed good food. The women were undoubtedly very good cooks and one festivity I would like to have attended was one of the traditional "last day of school dinners." That sounds like good food unlimited and in those days much of the food was home grown and definitely home cooked. These delightful recipes have been collected from old friends and fine cooks around Wayside, where my roots are, in southeastern Kansas, the spot where the Ingalls family of *The Little House on the Prairie* stories spent a year before moving on. I recommend this book for simple enjoyment and hope to try my hand some day with some of the recipes. Don't know if I can use my microwave oven or not.

— Bill Kurtis, Jr.

WBBM (CBS) CHICAGO
Television News Anchorman

6

CONTENTS

Preface

This book of recipes is dedicated to the people of Wayside, Kansas, and its surrounding area. Many of the recipes have been handed down from one generation to the next. Where necessary, modern-day ingredients have been substituted. Some of the recipes are newer family favorites from the great-great granddaughters of Wayside pioneer women, but all have met the test of time, as evidenced by the way the food prepared from them was consumed at the bountiful community dinners such as the last-day-of-school basket dinners, church functions, wedding feasts, patriotic affairs, and other gatherings and get-togethers. These occasions brought people together and sent them away overly satisfied and happy. No one could forget those delicious dishes—they were made with lots of love and plenty of pride.

In the early and middle nineteenth century, the area now called Wayside in southeastern Kansas was the frontier—inhabited by Indians, buffaloes and coyotes, was only to be crossed to get to the mountains or on to California.

The earliest known settler in the community was William Flanagan, who walked here from Pennsylvania in 1869. The Ingalls family also arrived in the late summer of 1869 and settled on 160 acres two miles east of present-day Wayside.

The community of Wayside was petitioned and established on May 16, 1887, on land homesteaded by Edward Barbour,

Mary Kristin, granddaughter of Bill and Wilma Kurtis, demonstrates how bread was once toasted in the fireplace.

8

who had obtained land grant signed by Ulysses S. Grant on December 6, 1871. Wayside is located fourteen miles southwest of Independence, Kansas, and ten miles northeast of Caney, Kansas, which is located on the Kansas-Oklahoma line. Three names were suggested for the new town. They were Corn, Hallsville and Wayside.

The Wayside community originally was settled by people seeking land. It was richly endowed by nature, with excellent soil, some timber, beautiful wide-open spaces and wonderful windswept prairie grasses that carpeted the land.

From the early days of settlement to the present time, many people earned and still earn their livelihood by farming or by the livestock raising.

Not only has nature been good to the Wayside area by its surface assets, but it happened to be located on a large oil field. The first well was drilled in 1890 and many wells were drilled from 1902 to 1904. Oil is produced from a level about 700 feet below the surface. Many millions of barrels of oil have been produced, but as much oil probably still remains in the ground as has been taken out. Although the present-day population of Wayside numbers only twenty-seven people, at one time during the oil boom there were between a thousand and fifteen hundred people living here.

It is interesting to note that one of the former owners of the "Little House on the Prairie Site," Lillian Jones Horton, came to Wayside in a covered wagon at the age of three weeks in 1884. She was my mother.

This brief history of the Wayside area is provided to give the reader an idea of the environment during which many of the recipes were developed.

Cooking is an art and can really be lots of fun. The more one cooks, the better cook one becomes. The recipes this book contains come from long-ago country kitchens where the aroma of hot pies, cookies, cakes, candy, biscuits, bread, buns and other homemade tasty treats caused lots of sniffin' and lip-smackin'. May their aroma drift out of the past and into your kitchen for you and your family and friends to enjoy as much as we have throughout the years. So enjoy and good eating to one and all.

My thanks to Mrs. Ivan Bowersock and to Doris Horton for furnishing some of the historical facts, dates, and names from early Wayside; to Margaret Clement for researching the site of the Ingallses Kansas home and giving me, as well as others, inspiration to look around us and study our own home territory; to Emporia Kansas State College *Spotlight* publication photographer David Stormont for furnishing some of the "Little House Site" photographs; to my son Bill Kurtis for the Wayside scene (back cover) he captured on film; and to my daughter, Jean Kurtis Schodorf, for the colorful "Little Post Office" painting she captured on canvas.

— *Wilma Kurtis 1978*

Bill and Wilma Kurtis, proud owners of the famous "Little House on the Prairie" site. Bill, a retired U.S. Marine Corps Brigadier General, is now an oil man and raises cattle on the Kurtis's ranch near Wayside.

"The Little House on the Prairie" Site

Laura Ingalls Wilder's books including *Little House on the Prairie,* portray the life of the Ingalls family—Charles (Pa), his wife Caroline (Ma), and their three daughters Mary, Laura (who wrote the books), and baby Carrie—who moved west in the 1800s.

The books are filled with true-life stories of the Ingalls family when the western lands were being opened to settlers. The house Laura Ingalls Wilder so vividly portrays in her book *Little House on the Prairie,* stood in an area now known as Wayside, Kansas. Today a large tract of that very land is owned and operated as a cattle- and oil-producing area by Brigadier General William A. Kurtis, USMC Retired, and his wife Wilma.

Wilma, who was born in Wayside, inherited the original farm from her family, and her husband Bill bought the rest of the land throughout the years. The Montgomery County (Kansas) Historical Society conducted extensive research and located the foundation of the original house on the prairie, the barn, fireplace, and the well that Charles Ingalls dug for his family. The water is still good, but slightly gassy. Wayside is an oil-and gas-producing area, although the first oil wells weren't drilled on the farm until long after the Ingallses moved away.

The book, *Little House on the Prairie* describes the land— there are many springs, and the native prairie grass is still here, the big and little bluestem, Indian grass, purpletop,

The "Little House on the Prairie" site in Wayside, Kansas, where the Ingalls family once lived.

Photo: David Stormont

side oats grama and buffalo grass. There are also bluffs which are mentioned in the book as well as the Indian campground, and some traces of the old road the Indians, and later the settlers, used to go into Indian territory. As for the "Little House" location, it's attractive and rolling, green in the summer, and brown in the winter. And when the train goes through, especially about four a.m., you can hear the coyotes howl.

The Ingallses had two western mustangs named Pet and Patty, which pulled their covered wagon over the prairie. Mustangs are small, like oversized ponies, and the books described them as "strong as mules and gentle as kittens." Once at the farm the Kurtises dug up an old horseshoe of rather small size that may have belonged to one of the Ingallses horses.

Wilma's mother, Lillian Jones Horton, was three weeks old when her parents came to Wayside in 1884 via covered wagon from Missouri. When Lillian was little, her mother (Wilma's grandmother) was often ill, and Lillian would tell her daughter Wilma how she remembered "Old Doc Tann" as he was called, coming down from the hill north of Wayside to call on her mother with his little black bag. Lillian and her little brother were frightened of him, and they would hide behind a door and peek around. Dr. George Tann ("Dr. Tan" in the *Little House* book) was the Ingalls's doctor and is buried in Mount Hope Cemetery in Independence, Kansas.

Before Lillian married Bert Horton (Wilma's father) she taught school near the site between 1901 and 1902 at Sunny Side school which was built in 1872. She had thirty-six pupils ranging in age from five to seventeen—classes from first to eighth grade were held in the same room—and she received twenty-five dollars a month for her teaching efforts. The Kurtises purchased the old school and moved it to the famous "Little House" site where they properly restored and refurbished it with the original desk Lillian (then Miss Jones) used, an old portrait of Abraham Lincoln, old students' desks, lanterns, books, a potbellied stove and other old school items used in the past. Tucked behind the old desk is the chair Lillian once sat in to face her pupils for their daily lessons. An interesting feature about the school is a door on the west side of the building that has an oval "looking glass" window that offers a charming bird's-eye view of the prairie.

A replica of the little house has been built by civic group volunteers of nearby Independence using logs found on the farm. The

Kurtises have visitors from all over the United States and from foreign countries who come to see the famous place. A huge sign erected on Highway 75 by the Montgomery County Historical Society that says "HISTORICAL SITE OF THE LITTLE HOUSE ON THE PRAIRIE" marks the spot.

To find where the ingalls family lived, take U.S. 75 southwest from Independence. Just east of Bolton corner or at the marker for Wayside, there are signs giving directions to the site.

When the Ingalls family moved to Kansas from Wisconsin, Charles was thirty-four his wife Caroline was thirty, and their three daughters Mary, Laura and Carrie were five, three and less than a year.

To Bill and Wilma Kurtis (both 1936 graduates of Emporia Kansas State College), Kansas and the plains are beautiful. They find it especially fascinating to study the history of the West and how the plains were crossed—particularly the Old Santa Fe Trail which extended from Council Grove, Kansas, to New Mexico. The history is rich and rewarding, like the land that seems to stretch out forever and melt into the sky. With a little imagination, one can easily picture covered wagons traveling over the prairie.

The "Little House Site" has become an historical family project for the Kurtises and their two children, Bill Kurtis, a television news anchorman for WBBM (CBS) in Chicago, Illinois, and Jean Kurtis Schodorf, a speech pathologist in Wichita, Kansas. They welcome one and all to come visit their land where once-upon-a-time-ago the Ingalls family lived in a little house on the prairie.

— *Anita Gold 1978*

Antiques columnist, *The Chicago Tribune*

The old Sunny Side schoolhouse as seen through the walls of the old cabin on the site.

PHOTO BY DAVID STORMONT

The interior of the old schoolhouse with some of its original furnishings, where Wilma's mother, Lillian Jones Horton (then Miss Jones) taught school in 1901. The school was started in 1872.

PHOTO BY DAVID STORMONT

Pioneers often whittled homemade toys for their children such as these. The little doll dressed in typical prairie fashion, wears a gingham sunbonnet and a calico dress. It was found in a covered wagon. The little horse on wheels has a frizzy little tail made of stiff string.

The Ingalls family had two western mustangs, named Pet and Patty, which pulled their covered wagon over the prairie. Mustangs are small, like oversized ponies, and the little house book describes them as being as "strong as mules and as gentle as kittens." Because such horses were of a small size, they would have worn small horseshoes. This small sized horseshoe was dug up by the Kurtises on the famous site and most likely belonged to one of the Ingallses horses, but no one knows if it was Pet's or Patty's. It's hard to imagine how many miles and miles of golden prairie land this little shoe plodded. It hangs in an honored spot in the cabin on the "Little House Site," and although its traveling days are over, it serves as a charming reminder of another time when Ma, Pa, Laura, Mary, and baby Carrie depended upon its use to get them over the prairie.

Carrie, Mary, and Laura Ingalls. Carrie wears a necklace of beads around her neck, that are no doubt the very ones the Indians left behind on the prairie and which Laura and Mary found. The incident is described in the *Little house* book and an illustration by Garth Williams shows the two sisters stringing the beads. But because there weren't enough beads to make two necklaces, only one string was made. Ma said it would make a pretty necklace for Carrie to wear around her neck—and so Carrie was given the beads. Mary (seated) and Laura (standing) wear ribbons around their necks that were crisscrossed and secured with a small pin. Note their gingham dresses that no doubt Ma made.

Picture courtesy of the Laura Ingalls Wilder Home and Museum, Mansfield, Missouri.

This is the famous Charles Ingalls and his wife Caroline, better known as Pa and Ma Ingalls. Note the pretty comb sticking up from the back of Ma's hairdo—no doubt a gift from her loving husband. Pa had an unusual beard. It hung straight down from under his nose and resembled a whisk broom. Ma's hands look strong and firm as if they could tackle any task—and indeed they did—washing, ironing, cooking, cleaning, baking, mending, lifting, lugging, and caring for Pa and the children. In those days a woman's work was "really" never done. Look at their faces—especially the eyes that are said to be the "windows of the soul." Look deep—can you see all the love?

Pa and Ma Ingalls's picture courtesy of the Laura Ingalls Wilder Home and Museum, Mansfield, Missouri.

Pa Ingalls played lots of good old tunes on his fiddle. One tune the family especially liked was "Old Dan Tucker."

Old Dan Tucker

I come to town the other night,
I heard the noise and saw the fight;
The watchman was a-running round,
Crying "Old Dan Tucker's come to town."

Get out of the way for old Dan Tucker,
He's too late to get his supper.
Supper's over and the dishes washed
Nothing left but a piece of squash!

Old Dan Tucker was a funny old man,
He ate his dinner in an old tin pan;
The pan had a hole and the dinner ran through,
And what was old man Tucker going to do?

Old Dan Tucker was a fine old man,
He washed his face in the frying pan;
He combed his hair with a wagon wheel,
And died with a toothache in his heel.

Old Dan Tucker came to town
Riding a billy goat, leading a hound.
Hound gave a yelp, goat gave a jump,
Landed Dan Tucker a-straddle of a stump!

Old Dan Tucker's still in town
Swinging the ladies round and round.
One to the east and one to the west
And then one to the one that he loves best!

Old Dan Tucker he got drunk,
He fell in the fire and kicked up a chunk;
A red hot coal popped in his shoe,
And bless you, honey, how the ashes flew.

And now Old Dan is a gone sucker,
And never can he go home to supper;
Old Dan he has had his last ride,
And the banjo's buried by his side.

Such tunes set toes a tappin' and hands a clappin', and woke up folks if they were nappin'.

This is Pa's (Charles Ingalls) famous fiddle that's portrayed so vividly in the *Little House* books. The family loved to hear Pa play his fiddle, and often after a delicious supper that Ma cooked, they would cozy round the fireplace and listen to Pa sing and play. Pa loved to play his fiddle both in and out of the little house, and often the night was filled with music that drifted over the prairie. Pa knew lots of good old prairie songs, some soft, others knee-stompin' and foot-tappin' loud. Sometimes, if you close your eyes and listen hard, you can still hear his fiddlin' on the Wayside prairie. Some say that the prairie winds are haunted with Pa's old tunes.

Picture courtesy of the Laura Ingalls Wilder Home and Museum, Mansfield, Missouri.

1 BEANS & POTATOES

Lucine's Green Beans

1 large can green beans
2 slices bacon, diced
½ cup chopped onion
¼ cup chopped green pepper
½ teaspoon salt
Dash pepper
Dash nutmeg
½ cup cream

Fry bacon, add onion and green pepper. Cook until soft. Add remaining ingredients. Heat through. Serves 4 to 6. Serve at once.

I know people who won't eat green beans fixed any other way but this. This particular sister of mine has a way of coming up with some of the best recipes you'll ever find—of course being an excellent cook (like Lucine) helps some too. W.K.

Indian-Style Kidney Beans

1 pound dried red kidney beans
¼ cup vegetable oil
½ cup minced onion
2 or more cloves of minced garlic
½ teaspoon grated ginger
½ teaspoon paprika
¼ teaspoon each of red pepper and cardamon
3 tablespoons lemon juice

After washing and draining beans, put in large kettle with 6 cups water. Bring to boil and boil 2 minutes. Remove from heat and let stand 1 hour, covered. Resume cooking, add 2 teaspoons salt and simmer. Add more water if necessary. Cook until tender. Heat oil, add onion and garlic and saute´ until lightly browned. Add remaining ingredients except lemon juice. Combine with beans and simmer until liquid has almost evaporated but beans are still juicy. Sprinkle with lemon juice and serve.

This is different, has a new taste, and I'm sure many people who don't like kidney beans would like this dish. W.K.

Green Beans Oriental

Heat slowly 3 or 4 cans (medium) of green beans while cooking the following: In skillet fry until brown and crisp ½ pound bacon (cut in 1-inch pieces).

Leave enough of the bacon grease in skillet to cover cooked bacon.

Add, over low heat, ½ cup sugar and ½ cup vinegar. Cook until sugar is dissolved.

Remove from heat and add 3 bunches finely chopped green onions.

Drain green beans and pour above mixture over them.

Carolyn's Scalloped Potatoes

Boil potatoes with jackets on; skin and slice thin. Put in buttered casserole with one diced onion and chopped green pepper.

Make white sauce of:

3 tablespoons butter
3 tablespoons flour
Salt and pepper to taste
1 teaspoon Worcestershire sauce
2-3 cups milk
1 package Pabst-ett cheese

Cover potatoes with sauce and bake in 350° oven for 20 or 30 minutes.

Rosa's Easy Scalloped Potatoes

Slice thin, 8 large potatoes. Melt ½ stick margarine and stir in 1 can mushroom soup, 1 can onion soup and 1 can cheddar cheese soup.

Mix well and pour over layers of sliced potatoes. Bake in oven 1 hour at 350°. May be baked on low in crock pot for 8 to 10 hours.

Early graters. The two larger examples are hand-made and were used in the eighteenth and early nineteenth centuries. The smaller example is a manufactured or "store-bought" type advertised in 1897 as a radish grater.

This nineteenth century cast iron and wood coffee mill is like the one Ma Ingalls used. Such a mill is illustrated in the *Little House* book. The freshly ground beans fell into a little drawer beneath the hopper, or top part, into which the whole beans were put. Some hoppers were shaped like open cups, while others (like the one Ma owned) had covers that slid open on one side so the mill could be filled. The turning of the handle set the inner gears into motion which caused the beans to be ground. Laura and her sisters would often grind the mill to help Ma with her chores.

These nineteenth century tin cups are exactly like those that the Ingalls used. In the *Little House* book, such cups are mentioned. And once Laura and Mary received bright shiny ones for Christmas. Long ago these cups were as bright and shiny as a new nickel, but because they are old, they've lost their shine to the elements of time.

This nineteenth century tin coffeepot and cup are like the ones that Ma and Pa used on the prairie. In the *Little House* book, an illustration by Garth Williams shows Laura filling such a pot from a bucket of water to help Ma.

2 BEVERAGES AND PUNCH

Ginger Tea

½ cup boiling water
½ cup milk
1 tablespoon molasses
½ teaspoon ginger

Mix the ginger and molasses together, add the water gradually, and boil one more minute. Add the milk and serve hot.

Hot, sweet, ginger tea was a favorite of Laura's especially on cold, chilly winter days when Ma would serve it to the family.

Honey Mulled Cider

10 cups (2½ quarts) apple cider or apple juice
⅓ cup honey
Dash ginger
Dash nutmeg
1/8 teaspoon salt
5 inches stick cinnamon, broken
1½ teaspoons whole cloves

In large pot combine cider, honey, ginger, nutmeg, and salt. Add cloves and cinnamon (tied in a cheesecloth bag, if you wish). Cover and simmer over very low heat for 4 hours. Makes 20 (4-ounce) servings.

Mulled Cider

2 quarts apple cider
¼ cup brown sugar
2 sticks cinnamon
1 teaspoon whole cloves
1/8 teaspoon ground ginger
1 orange, sliced and unpeeled

Combine ingredients in large pot. Simmer over low heat from 2 to 5 hours, or longer, depending on how spicy you like your cider. Makes 10 to 12 servings.

A Kansas Governor's Cranberry Punch or Tea

Cook 1 quart cranberries in 1 quart of water until berries split. Strain off juice. Add to juice 1 quart boiling water, 3½ cups sugar, ½ cup red hots (cinnamon candy drops), and 8 to 10 whole cloves.

Cook until red hots and sugar are dissolved. Strain again. Add juice of 3 oranges and 3 or 4 lemons to taste. These latter should be neither too sweet nor too tart. Dilute with 3 quarts of hot water and serve hot. Serves 12 to 18 persons.

I have served this many times and it is delightful. W.K.

Old tin pails such as these were used by prairie folks to gather blackberries, carry food and feed, etc. Small pails, like those in the foreground, were given to children as toys in which they often kept some secret treasure like a mysterious pebble or Indian relic they found on the prairie.

Nineteenth century pine knife-and-fork box with a center handle and separator. One side held knives and the other, forks. Back in the old days, spoons were held in separate containers called "spooners" of which there were various types made of glass and metal. Some made of glass resembled large goblets. Spoons were also kept in wooden spoon racks that hung on the wall.

Worn from years of use, these old-time wooden chopping bowls and mixing or "puddin" spoons, have seen better days.

3 BREADS & SPREADS

Ash Cake
Alice's Gingerbread Muffins
Banana Nut Bread
Carolyn's Icebox Rolls
Cheese Straws
Cornmeal Fried Mush
Cracklin Bread
Evelyn's Hush Puppies
Frank's Biscuits
Hoecake
Home-churned Butter
Johnnycake
J.H.'s Spoon Bread
Laura's Corn Bread
Lucine's Cheese Biscuits
Lucine's Hobo Bread
Ma's Vanity Cakes
Nettie's Raised Doughnuts
Oatmeal Gems
Old-fashioned Brown Bread
Dutch Honey
Old-fashioned Vanity Cakes
Pone
Sally Lunn
Salt-rising Bread
Lillian's Dutch Honey
Spider Corn Cake
Twelve Cinnamon Muffins
Wilma Kurtis's Wayside Oatmeal Bread

Ash Cake

This was made with a mixture of cornmeal, salt to taste, and water, which was rolled up in a ball, covered with cabbage leaves, and placed in hot ashes and small live coals to bake. It was often baked by settlers out on the prairie.

Alice's Gingerbread Muffins

1 cup sugar
½ cup sorghum
2 eggs
2 cups sifted flour
½ cup butter
1 ½ teaspoons soda
1 cup warm water
1 teaspoon cinnamon
1 teaspoon ginger
½ teaspoon ground cloves
¼ teaspoon salt

Mix and sift together flour, soda, and salt. Add spices, sugar, sorghum, water, 2 beaten eggs, and butter. Mix well. This is a thin batter. Bake in muffin pans at 350° for 10 to 12 minutes. This batter may be stored in the refrigerator.

Alice lives a couple of miles from Wayside and usually has plenty of young people around to enjoy such recipes as this one. W.K.

Banana Nut Bread

3 bananas
2 eggs
1 cup sugar
2 cups flour
½ cup shortening
1 teaspoon soda
1 pinch salt or ¼ teaspoon
1 teaspoon vanilla
1 cup broken up nuts

Cream sugar and shortening. Add 3 bananas, mashed. Add eggs and beat with egg beater. Add 1 cup flour and beat well— then add 1 cup flour mixed with soda. Add nuts last and mix well. Pour in loaf pan. Bake at 350° 60 minutes or when straw comes out clean when used as a tester.

Carolyn's Icebox Rolls

½ cup sugar or less
1 cake compressed yeast
½ cup lukewarm water
¼ to ¾ teaspoon salt
2 eggs
5 tablespoons melted fat or liquid shortening
1 cup warm water
5 cups flour

Crumble yeast in bowl, and add ½ cup water, salt, sugar, eggs (slightly beaten). Beat. Add shortening and rest of warm water and beat 2 minutes. Add half of flour and beat 3 minutes. Add rest of flour and mix well.

Cover with wax paper and cloth and place in refrigerator. Three hours before baking, knead and shape into rolls. Let rise at room temperature. Bake 10 to 15 minutes at 425°.

Carolyn says these almost melt in your mouth and I can attest to that. W.K.

Cheese Straws

Take equal amounts of flour, butter, and sharp, grated cheese. Rub butter into flour until smooth. Add cheese and a good pinch of cayenne pepper. Moisten with either egg or cold water. Roll out on floured board and cut into thin strips about 5 inches long. Dough may be chilled for easier handling. Put strips on cooky sheet, but not too close together. Bake in slow (300°) oven 10 to 15 minutes until brown and crisp. Watch carefully; they burn easily.

Cornmeal Fried Mush

½ cup cornmeal
2¾ cups boiling water
¾ teaspoon salt

Sprinkle cornmeal into the rapidly boiling water. (Use the top of a double boiler.) Stir constantly. When thickened, cook over hot water for at least an hour, stirring only occasionally.

Turn out into a loaf pan and chill overnight or until very firm. It is now ready to be cut into slices and browned in hot fat on both sides. This is especially good with maple syrup.

We used to have this mush periodically. Mother would set it outside on the back porch until it was ready. As long as we could use plenty of maple syrup it was a favorite dish. W.K.

Cracklin Bread

¾ cup cornmeal
1 cup wheat flour
¼ cup boiling water
½ cup brown sugar
2 cups buttermilk
1 teaspoon soda
1 teaspoon baking powder
1 teaspoon salt
¼ cup chopped cracklins (meat scraps left in the frying pan after the fat has been cooked out. These should be strained in a colander to be dry and crisp.)

Moisten the cornmeal with the boiling water and let stand for 5 minutes. Sift the soda, baking powder, and salt with the wheat flour and add with the rest of the ingredients to the cornmeal. Spread mixture thin in a greased shallow pan and bake in a hot oven about 20 minutes. When done cut in squares.

This bread was also made "prairie fashion" with just the cornmeal and cracklins mixed with salt and water; mixture was rolled in an oval-shaped cake and baked.

Evelyn's Hush Puppies

3 cups cornmeal
2 tablespoons bacon fat
Salt to taste
Boiling water

Add boiling water to dry ingredients. Cook until thickened, stirring constantly. Cool until mixture can be handled, then form into croquettes. Use approximately ½ cup mush for each croquette. Cook in skillet over moderate heat in 1 to 1½ inches bacon grease. This is a very old recipe and is still the best one. Very good served with fish or in place of corn bread with beans or black-eyed peas.

Frank's Biscuits

1 cup flour
2 teaspoons baking powder
2 tablespoons shortening to each cup of flour
½ teaspoon salt

Mix ingredients together with enough milk so dough becomes sticky enough to follow the spoon around the bowl.

Turn out on board or waxed paper and knead gently for a minute. Use very little flour.

Flatten out to a thickness of about ½ to ¾ inch. Then cut said biscuits with cutter and bake for 15 minutes in oven of 400 to 425°. Remove from oven and attempt the eating.

Secret of light fluffy biscuits: Place biscuits close together in pan so they have no place to go but up.

Hoecake

Scald 1 quart of Indian meal in enough water to make a thick batter; add a teaspoon salt, 1 teaspoon molasses, and 2 teaspoons butter. Bake on a hoe before the fire or in a greased baking pan at 350° in the oven. This makes delicious, hot corn bread like Ma Ingalls made. If you use a hoe to bake it on (like old-time prairie settlers did) make sure it's properly cleaned and greased so the bread won't stick. The hoecake was placed upon the blade of a cornfield or tobacco hilling hoe, with the shank of the hoe down, and set before the live coals. The hoe's long handle protected folks from getting too near the fire. The following is an old traditional folk song about such a cake. It was a lively fiddlin' tune.

De hen an' de chickens went to roos'
De hawk flew down an' bit de goos'
He bit de ol' hen in de bac'
I do b'lieve dat am a fac'.

O Jinnie git yo' hoe cake don' ma dear,
O Jinnie git yo' hoe cake don'.

As I was gwine 'long down de road,
'Pon a stump dar sot a toad,
De toad he winked to tadpole's daughter
An' kicked a big frog in de water.

O Jinnie git yo' hoe cake don' ma dear,
O Jinnie git yo' hoe cake don.

Home-churned Butter

Get a Jersey cow! You can churn either sweet or sour cream. Put cream in churn and churn it until butter separates from milk—pour off milk (buttermilk). Remove butter from churn after it has turned, and place it in a wooden bowl and work remaining milk out of butter with a wooden paddle by pressing it with the paddle to get out as much buttermilk as possible. If butter is too soft to work, cool it with ice water—butter can be washed with cold running water as it is being worked. After the buttermilk is worked out of the butter, mold the butter in a one pound butter mold by packing it into such a container. Then chill the butter until it is firm. Sour cream butter has the best flavor. (Any amount of butter may be made, even if not enough to pack into a one-pound mold, as butter can be packed into a small bowl as well.)

Homemade bread and butter is one treat that can't be beat.

Johnnycake

Put a quart of fresh cornmeal into a basin, add a heaping teaspoon of salt, stir into it boiling water until it is all moistened, then with your hands make it in cakes ½ inch thick. Bake them on a hot griddle rubbed over with a bit of pork fat or beef suet; let them do slowly; when one side is done turn the other. They may be baked in an oven for 20 minutes; or, put the cakes on an iron plate and slant it in front of the fire; when one side is done, turn the other. Serve hot; split them open and butter freely; they can be eaten with fried pork.

Ma Ingalls made plenty of these corncakes which she served with fat slices of crisp pork that she fried in her iron spider. The Ingallses also enjoyed such cakes split in two and spread with molasses. Ma would often give such treats to Laura and Mary, and such cakes are often mentioned in the *Little House* book.

At one time every country home had a butter churn like this old one that provided the family with plenty of fresh, sweet, butter for hot corn bread, muffins, biscuits, and other tasty treats.

These old butter paddles were used for working water out of butter after it was taken out of the churn.

J. H.'s Spoon Bread

1 cup corn meal (finely ground, white meal preferred)
1 quart milk
2 eggs
1 teaspoon salt

Place cornmeal in large skillet over moderate heat. Beat eggs slightly and add to milk. Gradually add egg-milk mixture to corn-meal, stirring constantly until mixture thickens and bubbles up.

Put generous 1 teaspoon corn oil or margarine in loaf pan and place in oven until pan is hot; distribute oil over bottom and sides of pan.

Pour spoon bread into hot pan and bake in 400° to 450° oven until it is browned on top and sides (approximately 30 to 45 minutes).

Serve hot with margarine or butter. Excellent with baked chicken or fresh green beans.

Better try this spoon bread and compare it with other spoon breads—you're going to like it better, I predict. W.K.

Laura's Corn Bread

1 cup cornmeal
2 tablespoons melted vegetable shortening
1 cup flour
½ cup sugar
1 cup sour cream
2 eggs
½ teaspoon baking soda
½ teaspoon salt

Mix cornmeal with flour, sugar, salt, shortening, well-beaten eggs, and soda mixed with cream. Mix well and turn into greased pan or muffin tin. Bake in moderate (350°) oven 30 minutes.

Lucine's Cheese Biscuits

Sift together 2 cups flour, 4 teaspoons baking powder, ½ tea-spoon salt, and ½ or ¾ cup grated cheese. Work in 4 table-spoons shortening and moisten to a soft dough with about ¾ cup of milk.

Press out on a floured board to about 1 inch thick, cut with biscuit cutter. Bake in 450° oven for 12 minutes.

Lucine's Hobo Bread

2 cups white raisins
1½ cups boiling water—pour over
   raisins and let cool.
2 eggs, beaten
2 teaspoons soda
1 teaspoon salt
4 tablespoons soft margarine
2 teaspoons vanilla
1½ cups white sugar
1 cup brown sugar
4 cups flour
1 cup walnuts

Add all this to the raisins and water mixture. Grease well, three 1-pound coffee cans and fill half full. Bake at 350°, 45 or 50 minutes. When done, turn out on wire rack. Bread will fall out when cool.

Just the name alone makes it interesting to make.

Ma's Vanity Cakes

Fill a thick saucepan about half full of lard or cooking oil and put to heat. Beat up a large egg and slowly add 3 ounces of self-rising flour (Laura's Ma probably used plain flour with a pinch of salt and baking powder) beating all the time.

When consistency is that of a stiff cake mixture, drop tea-spoonfulls on a floured board. Turn these over so they are floured on both sides and drop the little pancake into the hot fat. They will cook in about two or three minutes.

Lift them out carefully, let them cool and sprinkle with powdered sugar. You remember Laura and Mary liked these very much.

(This recipe is distributed by the Laura Ingalls Wilder Home & Museum, Mansfield, Missouri 65704. It is with their kind permission that it is included in this book.)

Nettie's Raised Doughnuts

1 cake yeast or (1 package dry)
1 ¼ cups milk
1 tablespoon sugar
4 ½ cups flour
½ cup sugar
3 tablespoons shortening
¼ teaspoon mace or 1 teaspoon vanilla
1 egg
¼ teaspoon salt

Dissolve yeast and 1 tablespoon sugar in lukewarm milk; add 1 ½ cups flour and beat well. Cover and set aside to rise in warm place about an hour, or until bubbles burst on top.

Add the following to the above: Shortening, sugar, and flavorings, well-creamed; egg, well-beaten, and remaining (3 cups) flour, and salt.

Knead lightly and place in a well-greased bowl. Cover and allow to rise in warm place until light, about 1 ½ hours.

When light, turn out on floured board and roll and cut doughnuts. Let rise again; then they are ready to fry in deep fat. Drain and roll in sugar or glaze with powdered sugar.

When Nettie Sewell says this is an especially good recipe and easy to make, I believe her - she has made plenty of doughnuts. W.K.

Oatmeal Gems

2 cups oatmeal
1 cup sour cream
Mix and let stand all day

In evening add ½ cup sugar, pinch of salt, 1 egg, ½ cup flour, 1 teaspoon soda, and ¼ teaspoon baking powder. Mix and put in greased muffin tins. Bake about 25 minutes at 350°. Makes 12.

Old-fashioned Brown Bread

Take 3¾ cupfuls of Indian cornmeal, 2½ cupfuls rye-meal, ⅔ cupful molasses, 1 quart milk, either sweet or sour; 2 even teaspoonfuls soda, dissolved in the milk; steam in a tin pudding boiler 5 hours; take off the cover and set in the oven to brown.

This old authentic recipe has been around for a long time and has been passed down from one generation to the next.

Brown bread tin of the nineteenth century. They were used to steam and bake delicious brown bread that was enjoyed by families for many past generations.

Dutch Honey

1 cup granulated sugar
1 cup sour cream
1 cup dark syrup
1 teaspoon vanilla

Cook sugar, sour cream, and syrup until creamy. Stir often. Remove from heat and add vanilla. Store in refrigerator.

Serve over pancakes or bread. Good on ice cream.

A family favorite - the kids never could get enough of it. W.K.

Old-fashioned Vanity Cakes

(like Laura's Ma made)

Beat 2 eggs very light; add ½ teaspoon salt and flour to roll. Take a piece of dough as large as a hickory nut, roll as thin as paper, cut and fry in hot lard. They will be done in a few seconds. Sprinkle with powdered sugar. They are crisp and light and may be rewarmed the second day in a hot oven a moment.

This is an old recipe that was passed down by country folks from generation to generation. Cooking oil may be substituted instead of lard.

Pone

2 cups cornmeal
2 cups wheat flour
1 cup sugar
½ cup melted butter
1 egg
1 teaspoon salt
1 teaspoon soda
2 teaspoons cream of tartar

Mix above ingredients with enough milk to make a moderately stiff batter. Bake in a well-greased pan at 300° for about 45 minutes or until brown around edges.

This was a dish that was prepared by the Indians as well as the settlers. It was also called "paune." It was shaped in flat loaves and pressed down and imprinted with one's fingers or palms. When it was brown around the edges, it was ready for eating with gobs of rich, home-churned butter.

Sally Lunn

2 cups flour
2 teaspoons baking powder
2 tablespoons sugar
¼ teaspoon salt
1 cup milk
3 eggs, separated
1½ tablespoons butter

Cream the butter and sugar together; add the egg yolks and make sure they are well beaten; sift the flour and baking powder together and add to the mixture alternating with the milk. Lastly fold in the well-beaten egg whites and bake at 350° about 40 minutes in rectangular cake or tube pan. This is an old country recipe.

Salt-rising Bread
(Prize-winning Recipe)

Starter:
3 medium potatoes
1 teaspoon sugar
4 cups boiling water
3 tablespoons cornmeal
1 teaspoon salt

Dough:
2 cups lukewarm milk
$1/8$ teaspoon baking soda
1 cup water
2 tablespoons melted shortening
$1/8$ teaspoon salt
Flour

Pare and slice potatoes. Add cornmeal, sugar, 1 teaspoon salt, and boiling water. Wrap bowl (in which ingredients were stirred) in a heavy cloth. Cover and allow to stand in a warm place overnight. In the morning remove potatoes and to the mixture add milk, water, baking soda, salt, shortening, and sufficient flour to make a dough just stiff enough to knead. Knead until smooth and elastic. Form into loaves. Allow approximately 1 pound of dough for each loaf. Form each loaf into a ball and then into a smooth long roll just a little longer than the pan. Work quickly and lightly to form loaves. Place loaves in well oiled or buttered pans. Cover and let rise until double in bulk. Bake in moderate oven (400°) about 45 minutes. Makes 3 loaves. Use pans according to size of loaves.

This favorite recipe of ours came out of the *Household Searchlight Recipe Book*. Ma Ingalls made plenty of salt-rising bread. W.K.

Lillian's Dutch Honey

1 cup cream
1 cup dark syrup
1 cup brown sugar

Mix together and cook until thick and creamy. Stir so it will not burn. Store in refrigerator.

This is my mother's recipe which used to make thieves of her growing family. W.K.

Spider Corn Cake

¼ cup flour
¾ cup cornmeal
½ teaspoon salt
½ teaspoon soda
1 tablespoon sugar
1 egg
½ cup sour milk
½ cup sweet milk

Sift the ingredients together and mix them with the egg well-beaten and the sour milk. Beat mixture well. Melt 2 tablespoons butter in an iron spider and pour the mixture into it. Then pour ½ cup sweet milk over the top of the batter, but do not stir it in. Set the spider over hot coals in the fireplace or set it carefully into a hot oven for about 20 minutes.

This early wrought iron "spider" stands on three spidery legs - thus its name. Laura describes such a pan in the *LITTLE HOUSE* book as having legs to stand on in the coals, and that's why it was called a spider, but if it had no legs, it would have only been a frying pan. Ma sliced fat salt pork and fried the slices in her iron spider. Lots of tasty treats were made in such pans, including Spider Corn Cake.

Twelve Cinnamon Muffins

¼ cup shortening
⅓ cup sugar
1 egg yolk
1½ cups flour
2¼ teaspoons baking powder
¼ teaspoon salt
½ cup milk
1 stiffly beaten egg white

Thoroughly cream shortening and ⅓ cup sugar; add egg yolk and beat well. Add sifted dry ingredients alternately with milk. Fold in beaten egg white.

Fill greased muffin pans ⅔ full. Bake at 350° for 25 minutes.

Quickly roll hot muffins in ¼ cup melted butter and then in ⅓ cup sugar mixed with 1 teaspoon cinnamon. These are some muffins! W.K.

Wilma Kurtis's Wayside Oatmeal Bread

2 cups boiling water
1 cup quick oats
⅓ cup butter or shortening
1 egg (this is optional, whether or not you want a richer bread)
½ cup dark molasses
2 scant teaspoons salt
2 packets dry yeast (net weight ¼ ounce per packet)
5½ cups all-purpose flour (about)

Combine water, oats, butter, egg, molasses, and salt. Mix well and let cool to lukewarm. Dissolve yeast in ¼ cup warm water, mix until blended, and add to mixture. Stir in flour to make a stiff dough. Knead well on floured board. Place dough in greased bowl, cover with a cloth, and set aside to rest and rise for at least 2 hours. Punch down, divide dough in half, and shape into loaves. Place in greased pans, 8½ x 4½ inches, cover with cloth, and let rise until double in size. Brush tops with melted butter and bake about 1 hour at 375°. Makes 2 loaves. Delicious toasted.

These nineteenth century tin kitchen cutters were used for baking. At one end is a handled, round, tin biscuit cutter. The gadget in the center is a clever invention consisting of five tools in one—a fluted cookie cutter, strainer, apple corer, doughnut hole cutter, and biscuit cutter. The other round object is a doughnut cutter that cut a doughnut with a hole in the center all in one operation.

This nineteenth century wood "coat 'n' cap" pegboard was made to be mounted on the wall near the door in a country cabin. Sometimes it was called a "peggy." Pegs, without boards, were also driven into the walls of log cabins to hold clothing and utensils.

Late nineteenth century cast iron sausage stuffer with a removable tin snout for inserting into sausage casings. Ground meat was packed into the top part and then the handle, which is fitted with an inner disk, was pumped up and down to force the meat into the sausage skins.

This old soap stick was used to stir homemade soap in huge kettles over the fire. Having stirred umpteen batches of soap in its day, the stick has a waxy feel due to long years of soap buildup that clings.

4 CAKES

Auntie's Applesauce or Fruit Cake
Banana Walnut Gift Loaf
Blueberry Buckle
Carolyn's Cranberry Crunch
Coffee Kuchen
Doris's Strawberry Shortcake
Faye's Mother's Apple Roll
Fresh Apple Cake
Gertrude's Banana Cake
Horn Book–Laura Ingalls Wilder
    Gingerbread
Ida's Date Loaf
Janann's Cream Cupcakes
Lemon-Orange Filling
Lola's Raisin-Cookie Cake
Lucine's Mock German Chocolate Cake
Mabel's Pecan Nut Cake
Mary Elizabeth's Orange Slice Cake
Mary Lou's Chocolate Sheet Cake
Nina's Ice Water Cake
Prairie Vanities
Strawberry Shortcake
Syllabub
Thelma's Raisin Spice Cake
Thelma's Sour Cream Chocolate Cake
Vanities
Wayside's Hot Gingerbread

Auntie's Applesauce or Fruit Cake

1 cup butter (may use part margarine)
3 cups hot applesauce (unsweetened Jonathans)
2 cups sugar
2 cups raisins (1 pound)
1 teaspoon cinnamon
1 teaspoon ground cloves
4 teaspoons soda in hot applesauce
1 cup chopped nuts
4 cups sifted flour

Cream shortening. Put sugar, raisins, spices, applesauce combined with soda in large sauce pan. Add creamed shortening. Heat to boiling. Remove from heat and add nuts and sifted flour, gradually, stirrring well after each addition. Pour into two 5x8-inch greased loaf pans. Bake at 325° for 60 minutes. Loaves are done when toothpick inserted in center comes out clean.

Do not add more flour, although batter may seem thin; if you like citron, ¼ pound may be added. I use this for Fruit Cake and add candied fruit in addition to the raisins. It is very nice and moist. W.K.

Banana Walnut Gift Loaf

¾ cup sugar
¼ cup shortening
2 eggs
1 cup mashed bananas
2 cups sifted flour
2 teaspoons baking powder
½ teaspoon salt
¼ teaspoon soda
1 cup chopped English walnuts

Heat oven to 350°. Grease 9x5x3-inch loaf pan. Mix sugar, shortening, and eggs. Beat hard until light. Add mashed bananas. Stir in sifted dry ingredients, beating smooth.

Add walnuts. Pour into pan. Bake 60 to 70 minutes. Cool on rack. This is a good one.

Blueberry Buckle

¼ cup butter or margarine
¾ cup sugar
1 egg
2 cups sifted flour
2 teaspoons baking powder
½ teaspoon salt
½ cup milk
2 cups washed blueberries

Make as a cake; fold in blueberries. Sprinkle with crumb topping. Bake at 375° for 35 minutes in 9x9x2-inch greased pan.

Crumb Topping

Blend: ¼ cup butter
        ½ cup sugar
        ½ cup flour
        ½ teaspoon cinnamon
This is an old-fashioned favorite that folks love. W.K.

Carolyn's Cranberry Crunch

1 cup uncooked quick rolled oats
½ cup flour
½ cup margarine or butter
1 cup brown sugar
1 can whole cranberry sauce

Cut butter into the dry ingredients until crumbly. Place half of this mixture in an 8x8- or 9x9-inch greased baking dish. Cover with cranberry sauce. Top with balance of mixture. Bake 45 minutes at 350°. Serve hot in squares, topped with scoops of vanilla ice cream. Serves 6 to 8. Another winner for Carolyn. W.K.

Coffee Kuchen

2 cups brown sugar
2 cups flour
½ cup margarine or butter
Dash of salt

   Mix with pastry blender or hands until butter is in small lumps. Take out 1 cup and set aside for topping.

   To the rest of mixture add:

1 egg
1 cup sour milk (May use ¾ cup milk and ¼ cup vinegar, let
   stand ½ hour)
1 teaspoon soda
1 teaspoon baking powder (Soda and baking powder may be put
   in sour milk and stirred)
1 teaspoon vanilla

   Stir and beat slightly. Spread the batter in a greased 10x13-inch pan or two 9-inch layer pans. Crumble reserved flour mixture over top. Bake at 375° for 30 minutes.

   Most kuchens are made with yeast dough and contain fruit—but try this one—it's easy and you'll like it. W.K.

Doris's Strawberry Shortcake

1 cup sugar
4 tablespoons shortening
1 egg, beaten
2 cups flour
3 teaspoons baking powder
⅛ teaspoon salt
1 cup milk
1 teaspoon vanilla
½ pint (1 cup) heavy cream
1 quart strawberries

   Cream sugar and shortening together; add beaten eggs; add part of flour, baking powder, and salt which have been sifted together; add part of milk; mix well and add remainder of milk and flavoring. Bake in shallow greased pan in 350° oven 20-30 minutes. When cold split in half and spread with whipped cream and strawberies; cover top with cream and strawberries.

Shortcake Dough:

2 cups flour
4 teaspoons baking powder
6 tablespoons shortening
¾ cup milk
    Rub shortening into dry ingredients with back of spoon. Dough should be soft.
    This is more delicious than any of the favorite apple dumplings, cobblers, etc. W.K.

Faye's Mother's Apple Roll

4 medium apples (or 2 cups berries, fruit)
1½ cups sugar
2 cups water
1 tablespoon butter
Cinnamon
    Dice apples. Cook sugar and water to form a syrup. Roll dough ¼ inch thick. Spread diced apples on dough. Roll up like a jelly roll. Cut roll crosswise into sections 1½ inches wide. Lay each section on its side in a deep baking pan. Pour hot syrup over. Sprinkle with sugar and cinnamon. Dot with butter. Bake in 450° oven about 25 minutes.

Fresh Apple Cake

1 cup sugar
¼ cup shortening
1 egg
1 cup flour
1 teaspoon soda
1 teaspoon cinnamon
¼ teaspoon nutmeg
¼ teaspoon salt
2 cups chopped apples
½ cup raisins
1 cup chopped nuts
    Cream shortening and add sugar. Add beaten egg. Sift together dry ingredients. Add last. Add fruit and nuts. Bake for 35 or 40 minutes at 350°. This is a winner.

Gertrude's Banana Cake

Mash 3 bananas and pour 4 tablespoons buttermilk and 2 teaspoons soda over and let stand while mixing cake ingredients.
Cream ½ cup shortening and
1½ cups sugar; add
2 beaten egg yolks
Add 1¾ cups flour and banana mixture
Add 1 teaspoon vanilla and 1 cup coconut and mix well
Fold in the egg whites beaten stiff. Bake at 350°

Gertrude Sewell's cake recipe should be good because she was one of the good cooks of Wayside. You could find Gertrude in the choir at church as regularly as Sunday came. W.K.

Horn Book - Laura Ingalls Wilder Gingerbread

1 cup brown sugar blended with
½ cup lard or other shortening
1 cup molasses mixed well with this
2 teaspoons baking soda dissolved in 1 cup boiling water. Be sure cup is full of water after foam is run off into cake mixture; mix all well.
3 cups of flour; add the following spices:
1 teaspoon ginger
1 teaspoon cinnamon
1 teaspoon allspice
1 teaspoon nutmeg
1 teaspoon cloves
½ teaspoon salt
Sift all into cake mixture and mix well.
Add lastly, 2 well-beaten eggs.

The mixture should be quite thin. Bake in moderate oven for 30 minutes (350°). Raisins or candied fruit may be added and a chocolate frosting adds to the goodness.

When Laura Ingalls grew up and lived in Mansfield, Missouri with her husband, Almanzo Wilder and their little girl Rose, Laura was famous far and wide for her gingerbread. In 1953, she gave the *Horn Book Magazine* permission to print her recipe, with wishes for good luck to all who tried it. Here, with the kind permission of *Horn Book,* is the recipe for all to enjoy.

Ida's Date Loaf

2 cups sugar
¾ cup milk
2 cups nuts
1 pound dates
1 teaspoon vanilla or orange flavoring
Lump of butter size of walnut

Cook sugar and milk until it forms soft ball in cold water. Add butter and dates; cook 1 to 5 minutes longer until dates begin to melt. Take from fire; add nuts and vanilla and beat until it begins to set. Pour onto a cloth wrung out in cold water; roll. Slice when cold.

Janann's Cream Cupcakes

2 eggs
1 cup sugar
1 cup heavy cream
1½ cups sifted cake flour
½ teaspoon salt
2 teaspoons baking powder
1 teaspoon vanilla

Combine eggs, sugar, and cream. Beat. Sift together dry ingredients and add gradually to batter, stirring after each addition. Add vanilla. Fill 8-cupcake-size pan with batter and bake at 325° for 20 to 25 minutes. (Can be converted into spice or chocolate cakes.)

Lemon-Orange Cake Filling

¾ cup sugar
¼ cup flour
⅓ cup water
1 egg yolk, slightly beaten
1 egg, slightly beaten
3 tablespoons butter
2 tablespoons lemon juice (fresh if possible)
2 tablespoons orange juice

Combine sugar and flour in saucepan. Add water gradually, stirring constantly. Add remaining ingredients and mix well. Cook and stir over medium heat until mixture comes to a boil and is thickened - about 7 minutes. Cool before spreading on cake. Makes 1 cup filling.

Lola's Raisin-Cookie Cake

1 cup raisins
2 cups water
1 cup sugar
½ cup shortening
1 beaten egg
2 cups flour, sifted
1 teaspoon soda
1 teaspoon cinnamon
1 teaspoon salt
1 teaspoon vanilla
1 cup nuts (or less)

Boil raisins in 2 cups water until liquid is reduced to 1 cup. Cream shortening and sugar. Sift together dry ingredients and add to creamed mixture alternating with raisin-water mixture. Stir well after each addition. Add vanilla. Bake in greased, floured, 10½x15½-inch pan in 350° oven 20-25 minutes.

This is a jewel of a recipe. I have used it many times when I have been having a "coffee." W.K.

Lucine's Mock German Chocolate Cake

1 white cake mix
1 package instant chocolate pudding
2 eggs
2 cups milk

Put all ingredients in bowl, blend well and mix 4 minutes at medium speed with mixer.

Bake in three 9-inch pans or one 9x13-inch pan. Bake at 350° or according to directions on cake mix box. Top with regular German chocolate topping or your own favorite frosting. Delicious; a very handy recipe.

Mabel's Pecan Nut Cake

Cream 1 cup butter with 2 cups sugar; add 1 cup sweet milk, 3 cups flour sifted with 1 teaspoon soda, and 2 teaspoons cream of tartar.

Fold in 7 egg whites beaten stiff and lastly add a large cup of pecan nuts rolled fine and sprinkled with flour. Bake at 350°. Makes 3 nice layers.

Mabel, who is Mrs. Jim Bell, lives in Wayside and has for many years. W.K.

Mary Elizabeth's Orange Slice Cake

2 cups pecans
1 8-ounce package dates
1 pound candy orange slices
1 cup coconut
1 cup melted butter (minus 2 tablespoons)
   Chop or slice pecans, dates, candy, and coconut. Pour melted butter over mixture and let stand while preparing batter.

Batter:

4 eggs
1¼ cup sugar
2 cups flour
1 teaspoon soda
½ cup buttermilk
   Beat eggs, gradually adding sugar and other ingredients. Mix well with first mixture. Bake in greased, floured tube pan. Bake at 325° for 2 hours or until done. A large cake and good.

Mary Lou's Chocolate Sheet Cake

Sift: 2 cups flour and 2 cups sugar
Bring to boil in pan:
1 stick margarine and ½ cup vegetable shortening
4 tablespoons cocoa, 1 cup cold water
Pour over flour mixture and mix well. Add ½ cup buttermilk or
(1½ teaspoons vinegar with ½ cup sweet milk)
Add: 1 teaspoon vanilla
      1 teaspoon cinnamon
      1 teaspoon soda and 2 whole eggs
Mix well and pour into well-greased broiler pan
Bake 20 minutes at 400°
Icing: Bring to boil
      1 stick margarine
      5 tablespoons milk and 4 tablespoons cocoa
Add: 1 box powdered sugar
      1 teaspoon vanilla
      1 cup nuts
   Pour over hot cake. Work quickly as the frosting sets up fast. Everybody's favorite.

Nina's Ice Water Cake

½ cup vegetable shortening
2 cups white sugar
1 teaspoon vanilla
3½ cups sifted cake flour
3 teaspoons baking powder
¾ teaspoon salt
1½ cups ice water
4 egg whites beaten stiff, but not dry

Cream shortening and sugar until light and fluffy. Add vanilla. Sift together four times; flour, baking powder, and salt. Alternately add to the shortening mixture, 1½ cups ice water and sifted ingredients. Beat until smooth. Fold in beaten egg whites. Bake in 3 greased and floured 8-inch layer pans, 30 minutes at 350°.

When cool put layers together with lemon filling and ice with "Fluffy White Icing."

Fluffy White Icing

Combine in top of double boiler: 1 egg white, ⅔ cup granulated sugar, ¼ cup white corn syrup, 3 tablespoons water, ¼ teaspoon salt, ⅛ teaspoon cream of tartar.

Place over boiling water and beat with electric mixer until mixture is light and fluffy and will stand in peaks. Remove from fire; add 1 teaspoon vanilla and continue beating until thick enough to spread.

I can say without reservation that this is the most delectable cake I ever ate. Of course Nina Jones (my aunt) was a super cook. She always came to all the community affairs with a basket full of her specialties. W.K.

Prairie Vanities

Two eggs, butter size of a walnut, 1 tablespoon sugar, enough flour to make very stiff. Take a piece size of a walnut and roll very thin. Fry in hot fat. When done sprinkle with powdered sugar and cinnamon.

Strawberry Shortcake

⅓ cup flour
4 teaspoons baking powder
4 tablespoons sugar
⅔ teaspoon salt
8 tablespoons shortening
⅔ cup milk
1 egg
4 cups berries

Sift flour with baking powder, sugar, and salt. Cut in shortening until as fine as cornmeal. Add milk and beaten egg, stirring only until flour is dampened. Place on floured board and knead lightly 2 or 3 minutes. Roll or pat to ¼-inch thickness. Cut with biscuit cutter. Butter one round and top with another. Bake 15 minutes in 450° oven. Split, fill with sweetened berries. Garnish with ripe berries and whipped cream. Fit for a queen.

Syllabub

Whip a small cupful of powdered sugar into a quart of rich cream, and another cupful of sugar into the whites of 4 eggs. Mix these together and add the grated rind of a lemon and a glass of white wine or sherry. Flavor with nutmeg, if desired. Good on sponge cake or fruit.

This nineteenth century tin device was known as a "cream whip" or "syllabub churn" and was used to whip cream, eggs, egg whites, and various concoctions like syllabub which was an old favorite dessert. The inner bottom of the container raises to a point to meet the cone-shaped plunger with holes that fits over it. Ingredients were put into the container, the plunger part was inserted, and the piece was tightly covered. It operated like a churn, with one hand holding the C-shaped handle and moving it rapidly up and down through a hole in the cover, while the other hand held the container steady.

Thelma's Raisin Spice Cake

1 cup raisins stewed in
2 cups water to produce
1 cup juice
⅔ cups butter or margarine
1 cup white or brown sugar
2 eggs
2 cups sifted flour
1 teaspoon cinnamon
½ teaspoon ground cloves
½ teaspoon allspice
¼ teaspoon nutmeg
1 teaspoon soda
½ teaspoon salt

Drain raisins from the 1 cup juice. Dissolve soda in juice. Cream sugar and butter; add beaten eggs. Sift together dry ingredients and add to batter alternating with raisin juice. Add raisins. Bake in greased, floured, 10x13-inch pan at 350° for 30 to 35 minutes.

Thelma's Sour Cream Chocolate Cake

1 cup sugar
1¾ cups sifted flour
5 teaspoons cocoa
1 teaspoon soda
1 teaspoon baking powder
1½ cups sour cream
2 well-beaten eggs
1 teaspoon vanilla

Combine flour sifted with baking soda and baking powder to sugar and cocoa. Add sour cream, well-beaten eggs, and vanilla. Beat until well blended. Pour into greased, floured, 10x13-inch cake pan and bake for 35 minutes in 350° oven. Cake is done when top springs back or when toothpick inserted in center emerges clean.

Thelma says she has baked this little cake since she was a child and she never had a failure. She topped it with a fudge frosting, but it's mighty good with an old-fashioned, real buttercream frosting. W.K.

Vanities

1 or 2 eggs
1 pinch of salt
Add enough flour to make a stiff dough

   Roll very thin, cut out little rounds with a biscuit cutter or the open end of a small jelly glass and fry cakes in deep fat.
   Sprinkle with powdered sugar and then eat them and say "yum!"

Wayside's Hot Gingerbread

Mix together:
1 cup molasses
½ cup sugar
⅓ cup butter or oil
Sift together:
2½ cups flour
2 teaspoons soda
1 level tablespoon ginger
½ teaspoon cloves
½ teaspoon cinnamon
½ teaspoon salt

   Combine both mixtures; stir together well. Add 1 cup boiling water and hastily stir in 2 well-beaten eggs. Pour mixture in greased and floured pan. Bake 30 minutes in 350° oven. Cover with powdered sugar frosting. Will stay moist 2 weeks.

This nineteenth century pie peel or paddle was used
for removing hot pies from the oven. They are often
found scarred with burn marks which give evidence to
their long years of service. The end part of such a
paddle was tapered so it could easily be slipped under
a pie plate in the oven. Such paddles also served as
"seat warmers" for disobedient children to make
them "smart" for being too "wise."

Old-fashioned pie crimpers or jagging wheels. Such
objects were used for cutting pastry and for trimming
and fluting the edges of pies. The one made of tin
has a pastry sealer at one end. The other is made
of wood and has a bone wheel. Such gadgets were
made of various materials such as brass, iron, tin, and
wood and were sometimes combined with wheels
made of china, aluminum, or bone. In the past they
were sometimes referred to as "giggling irons." Some
fancy types of whalebone were handcrafted by seafaring
sailors on long voyages to take home to their wives or
sweethearts as mementos of their love.

I pity the pitter
Who pitted the cherries
And splattered her kitchen all red.
I pity the pitter
Who pitted the cherries
She should have pared apples instead.

Cast-iron cherry pitters, like these late nineteenth century types that were made to be clamped to the edge of a table, were used in country kitchens when making cherry pie. Some performed a safe but tedious task like the "Goodell" example with the tray and two hooks above it that pierced two cherries at a time when they were set in the tray's holes to keep them in place. The two hooks have pointed ends that swing down, pierce the cherries and force out the stones through the holes. The cherries were then removed from the ends of the hooks. In 1883, this device called "the Family Cherry Stoner" was described in an old cook book as being as nearly perfect as any machine could be, and that it seemed to be endowed with intelligence. The other type pictured is called the "Enterprise Cherry Stoner." It has a cuplike top into which cherries were placed and a handle that turned a wheel to rid them of their stones. The cherries were supposed to come out, minus their pits, from a small chute at the end of the wheel, but unless you really had the right hang of it, you'd get a smashed up mess. If the handle was turned too fast, both the cherries and stones shot out like stones from a Roman Catapult and did a great job decorating the kitchen walls. Prairie folks who didn't want to fool with such gadgets, simply used the rounded end of an old-fashioned wire hairpin to pop out the pits by inserting it into the cherries.

5 CANDIES

Brown Sugar Candy
Ida's Christmas Divinity
Jan's Buttermilk Candy
Mildred's Cherry-Chocolate Candy
Molasses Taffy
Mrs. Bloomer's Remarkable Fudge

Brown Sugar Candy

¼ cup butter
1 cup white sugar
1 cup brown sugar
¼ cup dark syrup
½ cup sweet cream
 Boil 3 minutes and beat until cool. Pour into buttered pan. A favorite.

Ida's Christmas Divinity

2 cups granulated sugar
⅓ cup white corn syrup
½ cup boiling water
2 egg whites, stiffly beaten with ⅛ teaspoon salt
½ cup chopped candied cherries
½ cup pecans (may be subsituted for ½ cup green candied cherries)
½ teaspoon vanilla
 Boil together without stirring, the sugar, syrup, and water. When a thread forms when the syrup is dropped from a spoon, continue boiling until you count to 30. Then immediately pour slowly into the egg whites, beating until candy is thick and dull in appearance.
 Add rest of ingredients and pour into buttered pan or waxed paper. Cut into bars and wrap in waxed paper.
 Ida is Mrs. Bloomer and I can assure you her candy recipes are great and well worth your trying them. W.K.

Jan's Buttermilk Candy

1 cup buttermilk
3 tablespoons dark syrup
1 teaspoon soda
3 cups sugar
1 tablespoon butter
1 teaspoon vanilla if desired
 Cook over medium heat until mixture forms a medium soft ball. Remove from heat. Add butter. Beat until candy turns dull and immediately turn into greased pan.
 Use a good-sized pan to cook it - the soda makes it foamy. It looks like Brown Sugar Candy.

Mildred's Cherry-Chocolate Candy

2 cups sugar
⅔ cup evaporated milk
Dash of salt
12 marshmallows (regular size)
½ cup margarine
1 package cherry chips (6 ounces)
1 teaspoon vanilla
1 package (12 ounces) chocolate chips
¾ cup peanut butter
1 package large peanuts

Combine sugar, milk, salt, margarine, and marshmallows in saucepan over medium heat. Boil 5 minutes. Remove from heat and add cherry chips and vanilla. Pour into 9x13-inch buttered pan (cool). Melt chocolate chips in double boiler, add peanut butter and peanuts. Spread over cherry mixture and chill.

Molasses Taffy

2 cups molasses in an iron skillet
1 cup sugar

Cook together until it spins a thread - then add a little butter and a pinch of soda. Pour onto greased platter. Let cool until it is comfortable to touch - then pull - (oil hands with butter).

This is an old and simple recipe which helped the whole family pass many a long winter evening. The pulling is fun. Pull until candy is a light colored. Stretch like a rope, twisted, place on platter and when hard, break into all size pieces. W.K.

Mrs. Bloomer's Remarkable Fudge

4 cups white sugar
1 - 14½ ounce can evaporated milk
¼ pound butter or (1 stick margarine)

Cook to soft ball stage, stirring constantly. (Be sure to cook long enough.)

Remove from fire and immediately stir in two 6-ounce packages chocolate chips, 1 pint jar marshmallow creme, and 1 teaspoon vanilla, and nut meats if desired.

Pour at once into buttered pans; cut when cold. (2 cups whole milk and 24 cut-up marshmallows may be substituted.)

6 CANNING AND PRESERVING

Boiling Water Bath
Processing in Boiling Water Bath
Corn Salad Relish
Cranberry-Orange Relish
Miss Fairbairn's Strawberry Preserves
Green Tomato Relish
Mary Jane's "End-of-the-Garden" Relish
May Bloom's Beet Relish
Mom's Cranberry Jelly
Mother's Piccalilli
Mrs. Floyd's Plum Conserve
Ruth's Strawberry Preserves
Wild Blackberry Jam

Boiling Water Bath

The **Boiling Water Bath Method** is used for processing fruits, tomatoes and pickles. These are acid foods and can be canned safely at boiling temperature.

The United States Department of Agriculture says water bath canners are available on the market. Or any big metal container may be used as a boiling-water-bath canner if it is deep enough so that the water is well over tops of jars and has space to boil freely. Allow 2 to 4 inches above jar tops for brisk boiling. The canner must have a tight-fitting cover and a wire or wooden rack. If the rack has dividers, jars will not touch each other or fall against the sides of the canner during processing.

If a steam-pressure canner is deep enough, you can use it for a water bath. Cover, but do not fasten. Leave petcock wide open, so that steam escapes and pressure does not build up inside the canner.

Processing in Boiling Water Bath
(USDA Approved Method)

Directions: Put filled glass jars or tin cans into canner containing hot or boiling water. For raw pack in glass jars have water in canner hot but not boiling; for all other packs have water boiling.

Add boiling water if needed to bring water an inch or two over tops of containers; don't pour boiling water directly on glass jars. Put cover on canner.

When water in canner comes to a rolling boil, start to count processing time. Boil gently and steadily for time recommended for the food you are canning. Add boiling water during processing if needed to keep containers covered. Remove containers from the canner immediately when processing time is up.

(Home Canning of Fruits and Vegetables - Home and Garden Bulletin No. 8 from the U.S. Department of Agriculture can be obtained for sale by the Superintendent of Documents, US Government Printing Office, Washington, D.C. 20402, for 45 cents. The catalog number of this booklet is A1.77:8/9.)

Corn Salad Relish

½ dozen ears corn cut from cob
1 head cabbage, chopped
2 bunches celery, chopped
4 large onions, chopped
All cut fine
1½ pounds sugar
¼ pound mustard
¼ teacup salt (or less — go a little by taste)
2 quarts vinegar

Mix and boil 45 minutes. This can be bottled and used as desired. (Red pimientoes add color.) Follow USDA canning instructions.

Cranberry-Orange Relish

1 pound (4 cups) raw cranberries
2 oranges
2 cups sugar

Put cranberries through food chopper. Quarter the whole oranges, removing seeds, and put them through chopper. Mix with cranberries and sugar. Let stand a few hours.

This is a special favorite of mine. May be kept in refrigerator for several days, but for preserving follow USDA instructions. W.K.

Miss Fairbairn's Strawberry Preserves

Wash and hull 1 quart strawberries. Add 2 tablespoons lemon juice or vinegar (lemon juice preferred). Boil for 3 minutes, mashing berries slightly as mixture heats. Add 4 cups sugar and boil 6 minutes longer. Remove from fire and let stand 24 hours. Stir occasionally. Add lemon rind if desired. Put up in sterilized jars when cold. Makes 2 pints.

Green Tomato Relish

4 cups onion (ground)
4 cups cabbage (ground)
4 cups green tomatoes (ground)
12 green peppers or less (ground)
   Grind all and add ½ cup or less of salt. (Use coarse grinder.)
Mix and let stand overnight. Then rinse and drain. Combine the
following:
6 cups sugar
1 tablespoon celery seed
2 tablespoons mustard seed
1½ teaspoons tumeric
4 cups cider vinegar
2 cups water
   Pour mixture over ground vegetables. Heat to a boil, simmer 3
minutes, then can and seal. Follow USDA canning instructions.

Mary Jane's "End-of-the-Garden" Relish

9 cups cucumbers, diced and soaked in salt water for 3 hours
3 cups each of vegetables:
onions - diced
celery - diced
pimientoes - (both colors)
1 head cauliflower - diced
2 cups green tomatoes - diced and soaked with cucumbers

Dressing:

1 quart vinegar
4 cups sugar (or less)
1 teaspoon tumeric
1 tablespoon powdered mustard
¾ cups flour

   Mix flour and sugar together. Mix all dressing ingredients
together, heat until it boils up real good. Add vegetables - let boil
up again and then can. Follow USDA instructions.

May Bloom's Beet Relish

Chop 1 quart of cooked beets
1 quart raw cabbage
1 cup grated horseradish
1 cup granulated sugar
1 tablespoon salt
½ teaspoon black pepper

Add enough vinegar to moisten. Bring to boil and cook over low fire until tender. Can in pint jars and seal. (Follow USDA instructions.)

May was the daughter of Grandma Zenor and sister of Potiah. This family lived in Wayside for many years and a granddaughter, Rosa Mull, who just recently retired from our little post office, still lives there. W.K.

Mom's Cranberry Jelly

3 cups fresh cranberries
2 cups sugar
1 cup water

Cook cranberries and water until berries pop. Put through a sieve, rinse out the sieve and pan with a little more water (not more then half a cup). Stir in sugar. Put back to cook until it boils. Cook until jelly sheets from spoon. Chill until firm.

This was always made the day before Thanksgiving or Christmas. It is a bright, rather clear red and is very refreshing.

Mother's Piccalilli

Grind 2 large heads of cabbage, 5 pounds green tomatoes, 6 onions, 1 teacup salt. Put in cloth bag and let drip overnight. Next day, combine
3 quarts vinegar
3 cups sugar
1 box celery seed
1 box mustard seed

Do not heat. Stir until dissolved, then add to the vegetables. (Ground green peppers may be used also.) Bring to a boil and pour into sterilized jars within ½ inch of top. Put on cap; screw band firmly tight. Process in boiling water bath 5 minutes.

Mrs. Floyd's Plum Conserve

Rind and juice of 2 oranges
1 cup seeded raisins
1 cup chopped nuts to 1 pound plums
⅔ cup sugar
1 cup blue plum pulp or mixture

Cook as for jelly. Do not put the nuts in until the fruit mixture is almost done. Pour into sterilized jars within ½ inch of top. Put on cap; screw band firmly tight.

Ruth's Strawberry Preserves

1 quart berries stemmed (do not cut up)
2 tablespoons lemon juice

Set on slow fire and let juice cover berries, then boil for 3 minutes. Add 4 cups sugar and cook 7 minutes.

Let stand overnight before putting in sterilized jars.

Ruth is my sister. She makes strawberry preserves each year regardless of whether the berries are plentiful or not. She gets the home-grown ones and it is worth a special trip to her house to enjoy this refreshing treat. W.K.

Wild Blackberry Jam

3 cups blackberries
2 cups water
1 package fruit pectin
5 cups sugar

Mash the blackberries well after you have washed them and picked out any bad ones. Add water and fruit pectin. Stir until fruit pectin is dissolved. Heat to boiling. Boil 5 to 10 minutes. Add sugar. Stir until dissolved. Boil 3 to 5 minutes until thick, stirring frequently. Pour into sterilized jars to within ¼ inch of top. Put on cap, screw band firmly tight. Makes about 6 half-pint jars.

Blackberries grow wild in the pastures of Kansas. To go blackberry picking, better get up early in the morning, say 5 a.m. The main reason for this early hour is to get to the best berry patches before some other enterprising berry picker does. What a terrible feeling it is to arrive and find that all the big juicy ones have been picked - and it happens, or used to. Remember to insulate yourself with some long sleeves and gloves, shoes or boots, or leggings made of leather or canvas, if you can find such things, and of course long pants, a good straw hat, or cap to shade you from the sun that shines very brightly in Kansas. Oh yes, insect powder, put it in your shoes and dust your ankles to help control the chiggers. Believe it or not, you are now in business and ready to pick berries - and don't forget your bucket. When you get back home take a hot bath and again treat yourself for chiggers. I've never known why they are worse in a blackberry patch, but they surely are. W.K.

These turn-of-the-century potato mashers were sometimes
called "smashers" because of tasks they performed.

These tin dredge boxes date from the nineteenth century and were
used to hold flour and pepper. Usually the smallest of such containers held pepper and were called pepper boxes, like the one pictured on the right. Such dredgers came in both plain and japanned
tin, and some stood on little flat bases that projected from around
the bottom, while others did not. Meat dredged with flour, was
always enjoyed in the past.

This wooden hinged object is an old lemon
squeezer. A lemon was cut in half and
placed (one half at a time) between the two
boards. The utensil was held over a bowl
and squeezed. The juice ran out of holes
on one side of the squeezer.

Old slotted mixing spoons. The one with the horizontal
slots is a Rumford example that serves as a cake mixer,
cream whip, and egg beater all in one. It was patented
by Saltsman, April 27, 1897. The other with the vertical
slots mixed cake batter.

77

7 COOKIES

Chocolate Crisp Bran Cookies
Delicious Ginger Cookies
Five Dozen Ranger Cookies
Gladys's Persimmon Cookies
Josie's Sand Tarts
Nelle Hunt's Sugar Cookies
Orange Slice Cookies
Pineapple Drop Cookies

Chocolate Crisp Bran Cookies

2 cups sifted flour
½ teaspoon baking soda
½ teaspoon salt
1 cup butter or margarine
1½ cups sugar
2 eggs
1 teaspoon vanilla
1 cup Kellogg's All-Bran
1 cup semi-sweet chocolate chips

Sift together: flour, baking soda, and salt. Blend butter and sugar until light and fluffy. Add eggs and vanilla, beat well. Stir in the All-Bran and chocolate chips. Add sifted dry ingredients, mix well.

Drop by teaspoonfuls onto an ungreased baking sheet. Bake in moderate oven (375°) 12 minutes.

Delicious Ginger Cookies

1 cup white sugar and
   ¾ cup shortening creamed together
1 egg
1 tablespoon molasses (add to above beating well)
1 teaspoon cloves (or ¾) plus ¾ teaspoon ginger
1 teaspoon cinnamon (or ¾)
2 cups flour plus ½ or ⅓ teaspoon salt

Sift dry ingredients together; add gradually to above mixture, beating well.

With teaspoon, place small amount on greased cooky sheet; sprinkle a bit of sugar on top. Bake at 375° about 10 minutes. Watch 'em; they burn easily. Makes 40 cookies.

Five Dozen Ranger Cookies

1 cup shortening
1 cup white sugar
1 cup brown sugar
2 eggs
1 teaspoon vanilla
2 cups flour
1 teaspoon soda
½ teaspoon baking powder
½ teaspoon salt
2 cups quick oats
2 cups Post Toasties
1 cup coconut

Cream sugars and shortening. Add eggs and vanilla. Mix until smooth. Add flour sifted with soda, baking powder, and salt. Mix thoroughly.

Add oats, Toasties, and coconut. Mold dough with hands for it will be crumbly. Make balls size of walnuts. Flatten slightly. Bake on greased cooky sheet 10 minutes at 375°. These are delicious.

Gladys's Persimmon Cookies

½ cup shortening
1 cup sugar
½ cup raisins (I usually use 1 cup currants)
1 cup nuts
2 cups flour
½ teaspoon each cinnamon, nutmeg, and cloves
1 teaspoon soda
1 cup persimmon pulp
1 egg
¼ cup to ½ cup milk

Gladys says:
No special mixing. I finally got to using 1 teaspoon nutmeg only, also ¼ teaspoon salt. Drop by teaspoonsful on greased baking sheet and bake at 350° until done about 12-15 minutes.

Josie's Sand Tarts

1 cup butter
4 tablespoons powdered sugar
¼ teaspoon salt
2½ cups flour
1 teaspoon vanilla
1 cup finely chopped nuts

Cream sugar and butter. Add flour and vanilla plus nuts. Mix, knead and roll into small balls. Roll in powdered sugar. Mash on greased pan and make a thumbprint in each center and put on a dab of jelly.

Bake at 375° for 10 or 15 minutes. Take out and roll again in powdered sugar. These will melt in your mouth.

Nelle Hunt's Sugar Cookies

2 eggs
½ cup shortening
1 cup sugar
2 cups flour
¼ teaspoon nutmeg
1 teaspoon baking powder
½ teaspoon soda

Drop by teaspoonful on cookie sheet. Butter the bottom of a small glass and dip in a mixture of cinnamon and sugar before pressing on cookie dough.

Alice, Nelle's daughter, says this is a favorite of all her mother's grandchildren. She always let them eat all they wanted. W.K.

Orange Slice Cookies

4 whole eggs
2¼ cups brown sugar
2½ cups flour
1 cup nuts
17 orange slices (candy)

Beat whole eggs — add sugar. Continue beating — add flour. Mix well. Add nuts and orange slices (cut in small pieces). Spread thin in well-greased, floured pan. Bake 20 minutes at 350°. Cut in squares. Makes 2½ dozen medium cookies. Very chewy and yummy.

Pineapple Drop Cookies

½ cup shortening
½ cup brown sugar
½ cup white sugar
1 egg beaten
2 cups flour
1 teaspoon baking powder
½ teaspoon salt
½ teaspoon soda
   Sift last 4 dry ingredients together.
½ cup crushed pineapple
1 tablespoon lemon juice
   Drain pineapple. Cream sugar and shortening well. Add egg, pineapple; and lemon juice. Sift and add dry ingredients. ½ cup nuts may be added if desired. Drop on greased cooky sheet. Bake 12 minutes at 350°.

8 DESSERTS

Alma's Fig Fluff
Crystal's 24-Hour Fruit Salad
Marguerite's Glorified Rice
Raspberry Pineapple Fluff
Ruth's Cranberry Fluff
Thelma's Pineapple-Bavarian Cream
Wanda's Raspberry Dessert
Sunday's After-Church Dessert

Alma's Fig Fluff

1 package lemon gelatin
3 tablespoons sugar mixed with gelatin in 1 cup boiling water
1 cup cold water

Cool all until it begins to thicken; then whip until light and fluffy.
Mix in 10 fig cookies cut fine and ½ cup chopped nuts. Fold in ½ cup cream, whipped. Let set until solid. Serves 8. Serve with whipped cream if you like.

I had this recipe for 36 years before I ever tried it — now I love it. W.K.

Crystal's 24-Hour Fruit Salad

2 eggs
4 tablespoons vinegar
4 tablespoons sugar

Mix above and cook together until thick. Add 2 tablespoons butter. Then add the following:
2 cups white cherries, pitted and halved (drain cherries)
2 oranges cut in pieces
2 cups drained pineapple cut in pieces
Maraschino cherries, halved
16 marshmallows cut in quarters
Fold in ½ pint whipping cream, stiffly beaten, and let stand in refrigerator 24 hours. Serve on crisp lettuce leaf. Serves 8.

Marguerite's Glorified Rice

Dissolve 1 package lemon gelatin in ½ pint of boiling water. Add ½ pint of canned pineapple juice. When above is cold and partially set, whip. Fold 2 cups of cold, dry, cooked rice into the whipped gelatin. Then add a pint of whipped cream, 1 scant cup of sugar (or less), and salt to taste. Add any or all kinds of fruit, marshmallows, nuts, coconut, maraschino cherries, and vanilla. Let stand in a cool place 1 hour or longer.

Raspberry Pineapple Fluff

1 package raspberry gelatin
20 marshmallows
½ cup sugar
1 small can crushed pineapple
1 cup nuts (pecans or walnuts)
1½ cups whipped cream
20 vanilla wafers

Dissolve gelatin in 1¾ cups boiling water. Add marshmallows and stir until practically dissolved. Add pineapple juice drained from crushed pineapple. Chill until almost set. Whip. Add the whipped cream, pineapple, and nuts. Pour into pan lined with vanilla wafer crust. This is a very pretty dessert.

Ruth's Cranberry Fluff

2 cups raw cranberries, ground
3 cups tiny marshmallows
¾ cup sugar
2 cups diced **unpared** tart apples
½ cup seedless green grapes
½ cup walnuts
¼ teaspoon salt
1 cup heavy whipped cream

Combine cranberries, marshmallows, and sugar. Cover and chill overnight. Add apples, grapes, walnuts, and salt. Fold in whipped cream. Chill.

Turn into serving bowl or spoon into lettuce cups. Trim with cluster of green grapes. Makes 8 to 10 servings.

This is delicious and lovely to look at as well as to eat.

Thelma's Pineapple-Bavarian Cream

1 package lemon gelatin
1 cup boiling water
⅛ teaspoon salt
1 cup grated pineapple
1 cup pineapple juice
1 cup heavy cream, whipped
3 tablespoons sugar

Dissolve gelatin in hot water; cool; add pineapple juice and salt. Let cool until thickened, then whip until consistency of whipped cream.

Fold in pineapple and sweetened whipped cream. Let set in cool place until firm.

Wanda's Raspberry Dessert

1 package vanilla wafers (about 7½ ounces) or
  Equal amount of graham crackers, crushed
½ cup butter, very soft
½ cup chopped almonds (or any nuts)
1 cup powdered sugar
2 eggs, separated
1 pound red raspberries, drained (frozen, can use more)
½ pint whipping cream
½ cup sugar

Put ½ of wafer crumbs in bottom of 8x12-inch pan. Cream butter, powdered sugar, and egg yolks. Fold in beaten egg whites. Spread over crumbs. Sprinkle ⅔ of the almonds over.

Crush berries, mixed with sugar and spread on.

Whip cream, add ½ teaspoon vanilla and 1 teaspoon sugar. Spread over berries. Sprinkle with remaining almonds and wafer crumbs.

Cover with waxed paper. Store in refrigerator 12-24 hours. Serves 8. (Strawberries, cherries, blueberries, etc. can be substituted for the raspberries.)

Sunday's After-Church Dessert

½ dozen (more or less) bananas, nice plump ones, sliced. 1 tablespoon lemon juice and, if available, 3 or 4 juicy oranges. Sugar — perhaps ½ cup.

Just mix together and spoon into dessert dishes. When we were growing up this combination was a favorite for everyone — and come to think about it, it still is at our house. W.K.

Old cake molds of pottery and tin. Those with swirl designs were called "Turk's heads" because of their turbanlike appearance. Others had fluted designs, and still others were octagonal in shape or were plain. Those made of pottery are the oldest and they baked delicious bread puddings and other goodies.

This wooden mortar and pestle dates from the eighteenth century. At one time they were used extensively in the home for crushing herbs and spices. This one still has a faint aroma of garlic lingering from other days. Mortars and pestles were also made of iron, glass, brass, and other materials besides wood.

The larger piece is an early nineteenth century sieve made from various shades of horsehair (thus its plaid look) held taut in a hand-made wooden hoop to which the hair was attached. It was used for seeds and wheat. Often little hulls can be found stuck in the hair of such pieces which gives evidence of their use. The smaller piece resembling a miniature washbasin, is a home-made nineteenth century strainer or colander made of tin with holes in the bottom and a handle on one side. Back in the old days, these pieces performed invaluable services before modern inventions took over.

Late nineteenth century wire whisk and "Dover" egg beater. Such items were familiar to every old-time kitchen and are still used today.

9 FRITTERS, PANCAKES, & GRITS

Corn Fritters
Pauline's Baked Grits
Zesty Oatmeal Pancakes

Corn Fritters

1 cup flour sifted with
1 teaspoon baking powder and
1 teaspoon salt
2 eggs beaten
½ cup milk
1 teaspoon cooking oil
6 slices crumbled crisp bacon
2 cups whole-kernel corn

Combine ingredients in order given. Drop by tablespoons into 375° deep fat. Fry till golden brown. Drain on paper.

You might try these with honey. I enjoy them that way. W.K.

Pauline's Baked Grits

6 to 7 cups water
1½ cups grits
1 teaspoon salt

Cook these 3 ingredients until thick.

Add:

1 pound sharp cheese
2 eggs
1 tablespoon Worchestershire sauce
1 garlic bud, minced
1 stick margarine
2 tablespoons tabasco sauce

Put in a greased, flat baking dish and bake 45 minutes at 350°.

This is good for breakfast, lunch, or brunch — just about anytime if you like grits, and we do. W.K.

Zesty Oatmeal Pancakes

1 cup buttermilk
½ teaspoon soda
1 egg
2 tablespoons liquid shortening
1 cup quick uncooked rolled oats
½ cup pancake mix

Add soda to buttermilk. Let stand for 3 or 4 minutes; then add remaining ingredients. Mix thoroughly.

Bake on hot greased griddle until golden brown on both sides. Serve with ample maple syrup or Dutch Honey.

I enjoy these rolled oats recipes, especially, because I happen to be allergic to wheat, so anything with oatmeal in it I latch onto. Also it is high in fiber content which I consider important. W.K.

Various spices, so essential to cooking and baking, were kept in containers like this old homemade spice cabinet fitted with little drawers, and in this nineteenth century stenciled tin spice box containing six spice cans and a nutmeg grater. The fragrance of the different spices can still be detected in the little drawers and cans.

Cast-iron "Gem" muffin and corn stick pans. Such types were popular in old-time country kitchens for "delicious-from-the-oven" baked goodies.

In the past these old scoops had a multitude of purposes and were used in country kitchens as well as country stores. They were made of brass, tin, wood, sheet iron, and other materials, and they measured out everything from goodies to grain.

Old tin cookie cutters of various shapes. Their designs were endless and consisted of animals, fish, fowl, hearts, stars, geometric patterns, and numerous figures and objects. Back in the past, those that were shaped like devils were often destroyed or buried by superstitious mothers who didn't want their children eating such an image for fear the devil would get into them. Devil cookie cutters are very rare.

10 ICE CREAMS AND SHERBET

Cranberry Sherbet Dessert

4 cups cranberries
2½ cups water
2 cups sugar
1 teaspoon gelatin (Knox)
½ cup cold water
Juice of 2 lemons

Cook cranberries in 2½ cups water until berries stop popping; strain; add sugar and cook until sugar dissolves. Add gelatin softened in cold water; cool. Stir in lemon juice and pour into refrigerator tray. Freeze 2 - 3 hours, stirring twice during freezing.

To me, this sherbet never quite took the place of cranberry sauce, but it was a regular dish on our holiday table and it certainly was delicious and oh so pretty. Better try it. W.K.

Doris's "Six Three's" Ice Cream

3 cups milk
3 cups cream
3 cups sugar
Juice of 3 lemons
Juice of 3 oranges
3 bananas, mashed

Combine milk, cream, and sugar, and stir until sugar dissolves.

Place in ice cream freezer until mushy. Add fruit juices and bananas and continue freezing until firm. A tasty treat.

Horton's Banana Ice Cream

4 eggs beaten until light and fluffy
2 cups sugar — beaten in with the eggs until lemon-colored
1 large size can condensed milk
1 tablespoon vanilla

Mix all together and add about 4 mashed bananas to 1 gallon plus 1 quart of whole milk. This should make 1½ gallons ice cream.

(Follow directions on freezer.) Turn freezer until it gets hard to turn, then remove beaters from inside of can — scrape down sides with spatula — cover with wax paper and replace lid with the hole in the middle closed with a cork or something to keep out salt water. Repack with ice and let stand at least one hour before opening again.

For our family nothing ever took the place of home-made banana ice cream. We tried making other kinds from time to time but it never hit the spot like banana. Now the grandchildren are just as hooked on it as the rest of us. W.K.

Orange-Lemon Sherbet

1 cup sugar
5 tablespoons orange juice
2 tablespoons lemon juice
2 cups top milk or coffee cream

Add orange and lemon juice to sugar. Stir to help dissolve sugar. Add milk or cream. Pour into refrigerator tray. Stir occasionally.

Snow Ice Cream

Gather clean, fresh, fluffy snow and pack it down in a bowl. Add sugar, milk, and vanilla extract to taste. Mix well and serve immediately in cold sauce dishes.

This little fun thing is something children like to do and it is quite refreshing.

Wilma's Raspberry Ice Cream Cups

1 cup shortbread cookie crumbs
1 quart vanilla ice cream or ice milk (softened)
1 package frozen raspberries (10 ounces) thawed, use juice and all
12 cupcake liners

Fold raspberries into ice cream. In each cup spoon a layer of crumbs, ice cream mixture, more crumbs, more ice cream mixture, and a few crumbs on top. Freeze.

This is really good and a dessert that can be made days ahead. Good for large groups, too.

This early storage crock is made of pottery. A piece of cloth was placed over the top and tied around the grooved part with string to keep food in the jar covered and safe from insects.

This iron nineteenth century "seed-corn tree" was used for drying ears of corn that were impaled on its branches. They hung from rafters to dry corn for seed and were familiar objects in country kitchens.

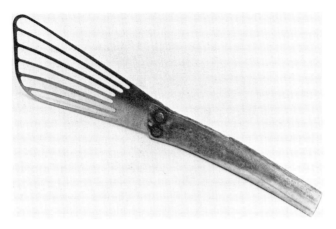

In the old days country folks never threw anything out, especially if it could still be serviceable. If something broke, they fixed it up in some way to make it do. Such repaired items were called "make-do's" and some, like this old batter beater, were amusing. The handle on this piece had been broken off at one time, and was cleverly replaced with a beef bone that was riveted on to take its place. "Make-do's" are popular collectibles because of their interesting repairs.

Eating utensils similar to those that the Ingalls family used. Note the three-pronged forks.

11 MAIN DISHES AND CASSEROLES

Aunt E's "Caserol"
Aunt Cordelia Jone's Fricasseed Chicken
Baked Chicken Croquettes for a Crowd
Baked Ham in Milk
Barbara's Barbeque Sauce
Chicken 'n' Dumplings
Dee's Mother's Stuffed Green Peppers
Delicious Wild Ricerole
Doris Ann's Broccoli Casserole
Ham with Pineapple
Helen's Baked Hash
Homemade Noodles
Ina's Mulligan Stew
Laura's Hungarian Goulash
Lela's Meat Balls
Lucine's Carrot Casserole
Lucine's Five-Hour Stew
Lucine's Lima Con Carne
Lucine's Sweet Potato Casserole
Lynch's Famous Chili
Ma's Rabbit Stew
Marjorie's Ham Loaf
Marjorie's Snappy Ham Loaf

Martha's Herb-Fried Chicken
Nellie's Good Greek Dish
Pauline's Scalloped Chicken
Potiah Stonecipher's Head Cheese
Prairie Chicken, Pheasant, or Quail
Prairie Pot Roast with Vegetables
Ruth's Hamburger-Corn Casserole
Scotch Broth
Sloppy Joe Sandwiches
Spaghetti with Bacon and Onions
Super Omelet Souffle

Aunt E's "Caserol"

Brown 1 pound hamburger; drain partially. Place in casserole dish.

Add:

1 package frozen mixed vegetables
2 thinly sliced potatoes
Salt and pepper
Can of cream of mushroom or cream of chicken soup diluted with ⅔ to 1 can of milk.

Bake at 375° until vegetables are tender. Sprinkle grated cheese over the top and cook another 5 minutes. Serve with hot rolls and green salad.

Aunt Cordelia Jones's Fricasseed Chicken

Cut large dressed fryer or young hen in pieces. Sprinkle with salt and pepper; dip in flour until covered and brown in hot fat.

Place browned chicken in roasting pan and add 2 cups milk. Cook in moderate or low temperature oven for 1 hour, or until tender. Remove chicken. Thicken broth with flour and pour over chicken before serving.

If Aunt Cordie fixed this you can be sure it would be delectable, so you might want to try it. W.K.

Baked Chicken Croquettes for a Crowd

1 quart thick white sauce
1 medium onion, grated
¾ cup chopped parsley
3 cups cooked rice
1 pint (2 cups) chicken broth
Juice of 1 lemon
3 5-pound stewing chickens cooked, then meat coarsely ground

Season broth to taste, combine all ingredients. Form into croquettes; roll in bread crumbs that have been browned in butter.

Bake 40 minutes at 350°. Serve piping hot. This makes 35 to 40 croquettes, and will serve 15 to 20 people, depending on the size croquettes. Usually a serving consists of two or three.

Baked Ham in Milk

Bake thick slice of ham in water until almost done — 20 to 30 minutes. Drain off water. Add the milk and baste often. Use the milk to make gravy.

Barbara's Barbeque Sauce

2 tablespoons sugar
1 tablespoons salt
¼ teaspoon pepper
2¼ teaspoons chili powder
1½ teaspoons curry powder
¼ teaspoons garlic salt
1 tablespoon grated lemon peel
6 tablespoons freshly squeezed lemon juice
6 tablespoons Worcestershire sauce
2¼ cups catsup
3¾ cups water

Combine ingredients, blending well. Bring to a boil and briskly simmer, uncovered, over medium heat for 20 minutes or until reduced to about 4 cups. Sauce should be thick enough to cling to meat or poultry.

I don't know who Barbara is for she is a mysterious person who at one time probably lived out on the prairie in Wayside. I have used her recipe for many years and it is an excellent tasting sauce. This is one thing I bottle and give to my neighbors occasionally. So thanks to Barbara the mystery lady. W.K.

Chicken 'n' Dumplings

Select a plump, 3½- to 5-pound hen. Place in kettle and top with water. Add 2 teaspoons salt; cover and cook slowly for about two hours, or until fork tender. Onion, celery, parsley, carrot, pepper, and thyme may be added according to preference.

Before meat completes cooking, mix ingredients for dumplings.

Dumplings:
1 cup flour
½ teaspoon salt
2 teaspoons baking powder
½ cup milk
1 egg

Remove cooked chicken from broth and cut in serving pieces. Keep warm. Drop dumpling mixture by spoonfuls in boiling broth. Cover so steam cannot escape and cook 15 minutes. Serve with cut-up chicken, with or without broth. Serves 6.

Dee's Mother's Stuffed Green Peppers

Brown 1 pound lean ground beef in 1 tablespoon cooking oil. Add 1 can tomato paste and 1 can water. Season with ⅛ teaspoon garlic salt, ¼ teaspoon Italian seasoning, 1 tablespoon minced onion. Salt and pepper to taste. Simmer for 1 hour.

Boil ¾ cup rice until tender in 1½ cups water and ¾ teaspoon salt. Drain (if necessary) and add to sauce. Fill 6 parboiled peppers.

Separate sauce for topping:

1 tablespoon butter, 1 can tomato sauce, and 1 can water. Heat to boiling stage. Spoon topping sauce over peppers and sprinkle 1 teaspoon grated Parmesan cheese over each pepper. Bake in 325° oven for 40 minutes. Yum — these are good.

Delicious Wild Ricerole

½ cup butter or margarine
1 cup uncooked wild rice (follow package directions for
   washing and preparing)
½ cup blanched, slivered almonds
2 tablespoons chopped green onions or chives
2 cans (7-ounce) mushroom stems and pieces
3 cups chicken broth

Put all ingredients in broth in heavy frying pan and cook over medium heat 20 minutes. Heat oven to 325°. Place mixture in oiled baking dish; stir, then cover tightly and bake 1½ hours. Serve with cold turkey and spiced peaches. Serves 6 to 8 people.

I have many times substituted brown rice for the wild rice—it is very good. W.K.

Doris Anne's Broccoli Casserole

1 packaged chopped broccoli
½ cup chopped celery
½ cup chopped green pepper
1 small onion — minced
2 cups Minute Rice cooked in
2 cups water
1 can of cream of chicken soup
½ cup milk
1 ounce Velveeta cheese

Fry vegetables in butter until tender and add other ingredients. Pour in casserole and bake 30 minutes at 350°.

This is a good-sized casserole. You shouldn't be without this recipe.

Ham with Pineapple

Put a nice thick slice of ham in a pan. Cover with brown sugar and 1 teaspoon cloves.

Place slices of pineapple over top. Also a handful of seedless raisins — pour in the pineapple juice. Bake at 325° for ½ hour.

Helen's Baked Hash

2½ cups (approximately) cooked roast beef
2 cups raw potatoes
1 medium-sized onion chopped

Grind beef and potatoes together so that the moisture from potatoes is absorbed by the beef. Add salt, pepper, and any other seasonings desired. Place in well-greased casserole and dot with butter. Bake 45 minutes at 350° or until top is crusty. Serves 4. This is such a good way to use leftover roast beef. It makes a main dish and is it ever tasty.

Homemade Noodles

Measure 2½ cups flour and put it in a mixing bowl. In the middle of the flour make a deep indentation.

Beat lightly 3 whole eggs and stir in 1 tablespoon melted butter. Put mixture in the middle of the flour. With a fork start a circular motion gradually working in the flour. The dough will be very stiff. Roll it out on a floured board until it is a very thin sheet. Let dry. Before the sheet is too dry, however, roll up in a loose roll and cut in thin strips. Now pull them apart, toss, and let them dry.

The noodles are now ready for use. Boil them in broth from chicken or beef, if desired, for 20 minutes.

Ina's Mulligan Stew

Brown 1½ pounds hamburger well
Salt—pepper, to taste
Dash of chili powder
4 medium-sized potatoes, diced
1 medium-sized onion, diced
4 medium-sized fresh tomatoes, diced (or 1 medium can)

Simmer until vegetables are done, about 30 minutes. Add additional liquid if necessary. Serves 4.

This is Ina Skinner's stew. She probably simmered it on a stove in the back of her General Merchandise Store which she operated in Wayside for many years. A nice lady. W.K.

Laura's Hungarian Goulash

½ pound bacon
8 medium onions sliced thick
   brown in bacon fat
4 pounds veal, cut in inch cubes
2 pounds pork, cut in inch cubes
   Cook on top of onions
Salt, pepper, bayleaf, Paprika and caraway seed
Add large can kraut (2-pound can)
Can tomatoes (2-pound can)
Boil 4 pounds potatoes until tender before adding to meat
Cook until well done
Just before serving add ½ pint sour cream

Wrap kettle in **red** bath towel for serving. Serve with good rye bread. Serves 8.

Lela's Meat Balls

2 pounds lean ground beef
½ cup chopped onion
¼ cup chopped green pepper
1 cup corn flakes
1 egg
1 tablespoon prepared mustard
Salt and pepper to taste
Enough milk to make ingredients adhere.
   Make into balls. Place in baking dish. Pour over meatballs:
1 bottle Heinz chili sauce
1 can whole cranberry sauce

Cover and bake in 375° over 45 minutes. When you have had all the turkey you can stand at Christmas time — this is a welcome change.

Lucine's Carrot Casserole

1 pound carrots (6 or 8 medium)
½ cup rolled Ritz crackers
1 glass Old English cheese
½ stick margarine
Salt and pepper to taste
Small bag Fritos

Boil carrots till tender. Drain and *save liquid*. Mash carrots; season with butter, salt, and pepper. Add cracker crumbs and cheese and mix well. Add enough liquid to moisten. Put in baking dish. Cover with crushed Fritos. Bake uncovered 30 minutes at 350°.

Even if you don't especially care for carrots, I believe you'll love this dish.

Lucine's Five-Hour Stew

1½ pounds cubed boneless beef stew
6 carrots, sliced 1 inch thick
3 onions, quartered
1 cup celery, cut in 1-inch pieces
1 can tomatoes, large size
3 medium potatoes (diced)
1 tablespoon salt
1 tablespoon sugar
3 tablespoons tapioca
1 slice fresh bread, cubed

Mix together. Place in a large casserole. (I use a small roaster.) Bring to a boil and remove from heat immediately, then bake in oven at 250° - **5 hours.**

This is a large recipe and part of it can be frozen. A terrific thing to warm up in a hurry — you are ready for any emergency to feed unexpected guests.

Lucine's Lima Con Carne

1 1-pound package large dried lima beans
1 large onion, chopped
1½ pounds lean ground beef
1 can (12-ounce size) tomatoes
1 can (8-ounce size) tomato sauce
3 teaspoons chili powder
1½ teaspoons salt

Cook lima beans until not more than half done. Drain and save liquid.

Cook ground beef and onions in a little oil until tender but not brown. Add to beans; add tomatoes, tomato sauce, and chili powder. Cook in covered casserole in 325° oven about 2½ hours. Add reserved liquid if needed. Serves 8.

This can be served with a tossed salad, hot rolls, and dessert — and you've got yourself a mighty good lunch.

Lucine's Sweet Potato Casserole

3 cups mashed sweet potatoes
1 cup sugar
½ cup milk
½ cup margarine (melted)
3 eggs beaten
1 teaspoon vanilla
　　Mix all ingredients together well. Spread in a 9x9-inch pan.

Topping:

1 cup brown sugar
⅓ cup margarine
½ cup flour
½ cup pecans
　　Blend first 3 ingredients until coarse. Add nuts, then sprinkle over potatoes.
　　Bake at 350° for 30 minutes or until brown on top. Serve with ham, chicken, or turkey. Serves 6 or 8.

Lynch's Famous Chili

½ pound ground suet
1½ pounds hamburger
1 medium can **red** beans
1 small onion chopped thin and fine
1 to 2 cups tomato juice

　　Render suet in large skillet. Add hamburger and onions. Cook until meat is nearly done. Add beans. Season with 1 tablespoon chili powder, salt, and pepper. Simmer.
　　More liquid may be added if necessary. Paprika added will give color.
　　Ben Lynch said you could always tell good chili by the kind of chef's cap the cook wore. It should be the tall kind, he said. W. K.

Ma's Rabbit Stew

Have Pa go hunting for a couple of nice young, healthy rabbits. When he gets back maybe you can persuade him to skin and clean them for you. Soak the rabbits in cold, salted water, overnight, or for 8 to 10 hours. Use ½ teaspoon salt to a quart of water.

Now you are ready to start your stew. Cut the rabbits up in pieces similar to the way you cut up a chicken and season with salt and pepper. Dredge each piece in flour and brown in hot fat. Cover, just barely, with hot water. You may add cut-up onions, celery, or parsley to your liking. Cover the pot and simmer gently until meat is tender. Do not boil. Remove rabbit from pan and thicken the drippings with flour as for gravy.

Dumplings may be dropped into the liquid or drippings. Cover them and simmer for 4 or 5 minutes without lifting the lid.

Rabbits abound on the prairie and the early settlers depended on them for meat. They are still hunted and caught in the winter by many people. W.K.

Marjorie's Ham Loaf

2 pounds lean cured ham
2 pounds lean fresh pork
Ground together
1 ½ cups bread crumbs
1 ½ cups milk
1 small onion — grated
Pepper and salt to taste (remember that cured ham doesn't need much salt)
2 eggs

Mix and mold into loaf in shallow pan or bake in two loaf pans. Cover top with 1 cup tomatoes, 1 tablespoon sugar, 1 teaspoon salt and ½ teaspoon soda — all mixed.

Bake 2 hours and 30 to 40 minutes in 300° oven. A too hot oven will cause loaf to brown and crust over, and it shouldn't do this. To test, stick fork in meat, and if juice doesn't run out, it is baked.

Ham loaf is wonderful either hot or cold. Cut in little squares, it can be served for snacks or hors d'oeuvres.

Marjorie's Snappy Ham Loaf

2 pounds lean smoked ham, ground
1 pound fresh pork, ground
2 cups soft bread crumbs
1 medium onion, minced
2 teaspoons steak sauce
Mix above together and add:
¼ cup prepared horseradish
1 tablespoon prepared mustard
½ teaspoon rosemary
½ cup warm coffee (medium-strength)

Mix thoroughly and pack into an 8x5x3-inch loaf pan. Bake at 375° for 1½ hours. Baste with ¼ cup wine and ½ cup brown sugar.

Marjorie Pence says this ham loaf may be made the day before and served cold. Or it may be arranged on a cookie sheet and reheated while other food is being prepared. Good with sandwiches filled with cream cheese.

This is a delicious ham loaf you really will like. W.K.

Martha's Herb-fried Chicken

1 3- or 3½-pound chicken

Place ¾ cup flour, 1 teaspoon salt, ¼ teaspoon pepper, ½ teaspoon each of thyme and marjoram in bag. Add cut-up fryer and shake well.

Brown chicken in hot fat (½ cup) in heavy skillet.

Place chicken in shallow baking dish.

Dissolve 2 cubes chicken bouillon in 1½ cups hot water. Pour in skillet; stir well, then pour over chicken. Sprinkle 1 tablespoon ground parsley and ½ teaspoon rosemary over chicken.

Bake uncovered in 375° oven 45 minutes or until tender. This is one of my oldest recipes and one I depend on. W.K.

Nellie's Good Greek Dish

Slice a layer of potatoes in a baking dish. Slice a layer of onions, then a layer of mangoes. Then slice a layer of weiners, add ¼ cup olive oil (I use a little less than ¼ cup) and nearly cover with water. Salt and pepper to taste and bake until tender, about 25 to 30 minutes at 350°.

Naturally the younger set goes for this, so don't expect to have any left. Serves 6.

Pauline's Scalloped Chicken

Step 1: **Cook** a fat 5-pound hen in 2 quarts water with seasoning. When cool - pull meat off bones and skin off meat. Put skin through food chopper.

Step 2: **Make stuffing:** Crumble 1½ loaves 2-day-old bread

Melt ½ cup margarine in heavy skillet

Cut up 6 sprigs parsley, 1 medium onion, 2 large stalks celery

Cook vegetables in margarine over low heat 5 minutes

Mix in bread crumbs lightly with fork

Grind cooked giblets and mix in

Add 1 teaspoon salt, dash pepper, 1 teaspoon poultry seasoning

Mix in 6 tablespoons chicken broth

Step 3: **Sauce**

Skim fat off chicken broth

Heat 1 cup skimmed fat in large heavy saucepan. (If not enough fat, make up difference with margarine)

Heat 4 cups chicken broth, 1 cup milk, together. Do not boil

Stir in 1 cup flour

Add broth and milk mixture, 2 teaspoons salt. Cook until thick

Beat 4 eggs slightly, mix in a little of the sauce, then

Combine eggs and sauce and cook over low heat 3 or 4 minutes

Keep stirring, add ground chicken skin as you take it off heat

Step 4: **Grease** one very large or 2 smaller casseroles

Put stuffing in bottom carefully

Pour over it **half** the sauce

On top of this put the diced chicken meat

Add remaining sauce

Toss 1 cup dry bread crumbs in 4 tablespoons melted margarine

Sprinkle on top

Bake 20 minutes in moderate oven, 375°, or until crumbs are golden brown and chicken is hot all through. Will serve at least 15 to 18.

Just because this recipe is long doesn't mean it is difficult. Read it through a couple times then you'll know what you're doing. A great dish for a group affair and can be fixed ahead of time and warmed through at serving. Serve with Perfection Salad. W.K.

Potiah Stonecipher's Head Cheese

Clean hog's head, (cut in half). Soak in salted water overnight. Remove and cover with water and cook until done. Take meat from bones. Grind or chop fine. Return ground meat to kettle. Season with salt and pepper. Add enough broth to just cover meat. Cook slowly about 15 minutes. Pour in crock and cover with clean cheesecloth weighted down until cool. Store in refrigerator. Slice to serve.

Potiah, also known as Aunt Port, was a daughter of Grandma Anna Zenor. Aunt Port lived to be 102 years old. I wish I knew how many pies she baked in her lifetime. W.K.

Prairie Chicken, Pheasant, or Quail

Cup up pheasant or prairie chicken as you would cut a chicken for frying. (Quail may be cooked whole or divided into two sections.) Soak game in cold water for several hours. Drain. Dip game in flour seasoned with salt and pepper. Brown slowly in several tablespoons of shortening in a heavy skillet.

Place game in roaster or baking dish; add 1 cup cold water to drippings in skillet. Pour over game. Cover.

Bake in slow oven (275°-300°) for approximately 2 hours, or until tender.

Since we now have cream of mushroom and cream of chicken soups - a can of either plus ½ cup of milk may be used instead of the water. The gravy is ready with this mixture.

This is the method Ruth Diver used to fix the game that Randall, her husband, brings in. He is an avid hunter and fisherman and has made regular trips hunting and fishing every year. Ruth has learned through experience. She says if she gets an old bird it may take all day before it is tender. W.K.

Prairie Pot Roast with Vegetables

Use a 4-pound chuck, arm, round bone, or rump roast. Season and brown meat on both sides in 2 tablespoons hot fat in large pan or roaster with tight lid. Do not add water; it will make its own liquid. Cover and place in 300° oven. Total roasting time will be approximately 3 hours. Vegetables are added in the last 45 minutes of cooking. Prepare and cut 2 each of carrots and onions and as many potatoes as desired. Arrange around meat; salt and pepper them; cover and continue cooking. If meat has not produced enough liquid, ½ cup water may be added with vegetables, but go easy if you want brown, crusty potatoes. Serves 6.

Ruth's Hamburger-Corn Casserole

1 ½ pounds ground lean beef
1 cup chopped onion
Salt, pepper, ½ teaspoon Accent

Cook the above until onions are tender. I usually cook this covered.

Add: 1 12-ounce can whole-kernel corn (drained)
      1 can cream of chicken soup
      1 can cream of mushroom soup
      1 cup sour cream

Mix well. Stir in 3 cups of **cooked** noodles. I use the crinkly kind (about 5 ounces or half a package).

Pour in casserole — top with buttered bread crumbs and dot with cheese. Bake at 350° for 30 or 40 minutes. This will serve 10 to 12. Can be frozen.

Scotch Broth (An old recipe or "receipt")

Two pounds of the scraggy part of a neck of mutton. Cut the meat from the bones; cut off all the fat. Put into a kettle with one large slice of turnip, two of carrot, one onion and a stalk of celery, all cut fine, half of cupful of barley, and three pints of cold water. Simmer gently for two hours. Put a pint of water on the bones; simmer two hours and strain into the soup. Cook a tablespoon of flour and 1 of butter together until perfectly smooth, then add to the soup. Season with salt and pepper to taste.

This late nineteenth century cast-iron pot cooked Scotch broth, soups, porridges, and was known as a "Scotch bowl" because of its bowl-like shape. The little ring that hangs down in front was used to hang the pot up when it wasn't in use.

Sloppy Joe Sandwiches

3 pounds ground beef (very lean)
Brown with 2 medium onions
Add:
1 chopped green pepper
2 teaspoons salt
1 clove garlic, crushed
2 teaspoons black pepper
1 teaspoon dry mustard
1 tablespoon chili powder
1 cup catsup
1 cup tomato juice
1 tablespoon Worcestershire sauce
Mix all together. Put in large pan and bake in 350° oven 30-45 minutes or until done. Can be thickened with corn flakes.

Spaghetti with Bacon and Onions

12-ounce package spaghetti
Prepare according to directions on package
Remove from heat and drain. Set aside pan
Fry 4 or 5 slices bacon (cut up) until **almost** crisp, with chopped onion (medium size) — add this to spaghetti. Also add 1 large size can tomatoes to which add 1 teaspoon sugar and 1 teaspoon salt plus an 8-ounce can tomato sauce. Some catsup may be added if needed.

Mix and place in 8x10 baking pan or large-sized casserole dish. Bake 30 to 40 minutes at 350°.

We use this hot or cold. It is especially good to take to a picnic. An old favorite. W.K.

Super Omelet Souffle

Multiply per number of persons to be served:
½ tablespoon butter or margarine
½ tablespoon flour
¼ cup milk
⅛ teaspoon salt
1 egg
Make cream sauce. Cool. Add beaten egg yolk. Then cut in stiffly beaten egg white. Bake in ungreased casserole at 350°, 40 to 45 minutes. (Add 1 tablespoon bread crumbs to every 4 eggs.) Doesn't fall then! Super delicious.

Early cast-iron "Dutch oven" with a removable folding handle. It stood on short, stubby feet in the fireplace and was used for baking a bread sometimes called "Fire cake," because it was baked within the embers which also were heaped on the cover around the deep rim for extra heat. Such pots were also called "Bake ovens," and Ma Ingalls used one in which she baked corn bread in the fireplace. In her book *Little House on the Prairie*, Laura Ingalls describes how her ma made the bread from cornmeal and water into two thin loaves, each shaped in a half circle, and laid them in the bake oven with their straight sides together. Ma pressed her hand flat on the top of each loaf, and Pa said that Ma's handprints were all the sweetening the loaves needed. Such bake ovens were also designed for camp use and could be set in the center of a wood fire without injury to the contents being cooked. The cover fit down snugly so that nothing could get inside. Some had removable bail handles while others had stationary ones.

Old gridirons like those used in the eighteenth and early nineteenth centuries. At one time they were common hearth furnishings. Some round ones were swivel-types that rotated on a center pin.

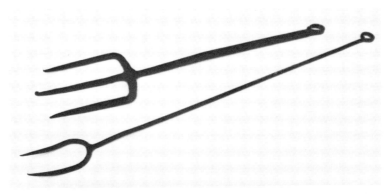

These wrought iron flesh forks were used for toasting and roasting over smoldering fires. Those with three prongs were called "tormentors" because of their resemblance to the devil's tool. Those with two prongs were also used for lifting meat from pots.

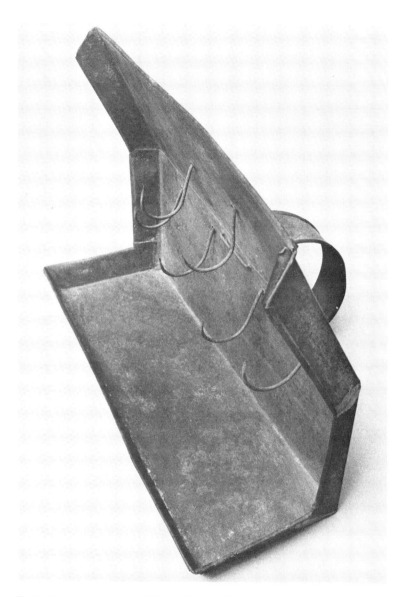

Early tin bird roaster. Small birds like bobwhites were secured or pinned on the hooks, and the roaster was placed on the hearth in front of the fire until the birds were done. A tray at the bottom of the bird roaster caught the drippings. Such pieces have a curved handle at the back so that they could be removed from the fireplace.

12 PIES

Piecrust (Dependable)
Alta's Pumpkin Pie
Doris's White Christmas Pie
Grace's Pumpkin Pie
Lucine's Fruit Pie
Mock Cherry Pie
Mrs. Braden's Curd Tarts
Mrs. Vandevanter's Caramel-Nut Pie
Old-fashioned Cranberry Tarts
Old-fashioned Cream Pie
Pecan Pie Anyone Can Make
Rhubarb Pie
Upside-down Peach Pie

Piecrust (Dependable)

(For 9-inch crust) 1 cup sifted flour
 ¼ teaspoon salt
 1 tablespoon sugar
 ¼ cup shortening
 ¾ teaspoon lemon juice or vinegar
 ¼ cup milk

Sift flour with salt and sugar. Add half of the shortening and work in quickly with fingers until mixture is like cornmeal. Add remainder of shortening and work in until the shortening and flour are about the size of peas. (This mixture may be stored and used as needed.) Stir lemon juice or vinegar into the milk. Add milk all at once and stir with a fork. If more liquid is needed add only enough to make dough soft enough to roll out.

Alta's Pumpkin Pie

4 eggs slightly beaten
2 cups sugar
½ teaspoon cinnamon
½ teaspoon nutmeg
1 teaspoon salt (scant)
2 cups half-and-half cream
3 cups canned pumpkin (solid pack)

Mix sugar, spices, and salt together. Beat eggs. Add milk, then sugar mixture and pumpkin. Bake at 425° for 15 minutes, then for 30 minutes more at 350°. (Never let a custard pie boil.) Makes 2 pies.

Crust for Two 1-Crust Pies

1½ cups flour
½ cup vegetable shortening
¼ teaspoon salt

Mix together until crumbly. Sprinkle with water to make dough hold together. Alta Riley has lived on Bell Avenue in Wayside for a good many years. W.K.

Doris's White Christmas Pie

Filling:
Soften 1 tablespoon gelatin in ¼ cup cold water. Let stand
Mix together in saucepan
½ cup sugar, 4 tablespoons flour, ½ teaspoon salt, 1½ cups
milk

Cook over very low heat, stirring until it boils. Boil 1 minute. Remove from heat. Stir in softened gelatin. Cool. When partially set, beat with rotary beater until smooth. Blend in ¾ teaspoon vanilla and ¼ teaspoon almond extract. Gently fold in ½ cup whipping cream, whipped until stiff. Make a meringue of 3 egg whites, ¼ teaspoon cream of tarter and ½ cup sugar. Fold meringue into the filling. Fold in 1 cup moist shredded or flaked coconut.

Pile into a cooled, baked pie shell. Sprinkle with coconut. Chill until set, about 2 hours. Serve cold.

This is an old recipe. My sister Doris makes this pie for our special dinners and has for many years. It is a delicious dessert and one might call it elegant. W.K.

Grace's Pumpkin Pie

1 cup canned pumpkin
1 cup sugar
3 eggs
2 cups milk
1 teaspoon cinnamon
1¼ teaspoons ginger
¼ teaspoon salt
1 tablespoon melted butter
1 teaspoon vanilla

Thoroughly mix beaten egg yolks, milk, melted butter, spices, salt, and vanilla. Fold in stiffly beaten egg whites. Pour mixture into 2 unbaked piecrusts. Bake for 15 minutes at 400°, then at 350° for 30 minutes. Pies are done when knife inserted comes out clean.

Grace Herring was a fine cook, and so was her husband John. The Herrings lived in Wayside and baked delicious treats at a time when mixes weren't around. W.K.

Lucine's Fruit Pie

Mix and cook until thick:
1 can sour pie cherries (juice included)
1 No. 2 (20-ounce) can crushed pineapple
1 cup sugar
2 tablespoons flour
2 teaspoons red food coloring (optional)
   While **hot** add one 3-ounce package orange gelatin and 1 teaspoon vanilla. Cool about 1½ hours.
   When cool add:
3 or 4 sliced bananas
1 cup chopped pecans
   Pour into 2 baked pie shells or about 30 tart shells. Serve with a dollop of whipped cream.

Mock Cherry Pie

   Mix together ingredients for 2-crust pie. Line pie pan with ½ of pastry. Chop together 1 cup cranberries and ½ cup raisins. Put into unbaked piecrust. Mix together ½ cup sugar, 1 tablespoon flour and spread over berries. Combine ½ cup water and ½ teaspoon vanilla and a pinch of salt and pour over flour and sugar. Put on top crust and bake at 450° 10 minutes, then at 350° for 30 minutes.

Mrs. Braden's Curd Tarts

Grated rind of 2 medium lemons
2 cups sugar
4 eggs, well beaten
½ cup lemon juice
1 cup butter or margarine
4 dozen miniature, baked, cooled tart shells
Crust:
3 cups flour
1 cup shortening
1½ teaspoons salt
6 tablespoons cold water
Bake 12-15 minutes at 450°
   Mix lemon rind, sugar, well-beaten eggs, lemon juice, and margarine together in top of double boiler. Cook, stirring constantly until mixture thickens. Remove from heat and allow to cool. Pour into baked tart shells; then eat and enjoy.

Mrs. Vandevanter's Caramel-Nut Pie

2 cups milk
1 cup brown sugar
4 tablespoons flour
¼ teaspoon salt
2 eggs, separated
1 tablespoon butter
½ cup nuts, chopped
1 teaspoon vanilla

Mix flour, sugar, and egg yolks and beat well. Add to hot milk and cook until thick, stirring constantly. Add nuts and vanilla. Pour into baked pie shell. Make meringue.

Meringue:

Beat the two egg whites until soft peaks are formed. Gradually beat in 3 tablespoons of powdered sugar. Beat until stiff peaks are formed, all sugar is dissolved, and mixture has a glossy appearance. Pile on top of pie, making sure edges are sealed. Bake in moderate (350°) oven 13 to 15 minutes.

Old-fashioned Cranberry Tarts

2 cups whole cranberry sauce or 1 can (16 ounces)
¼ cup raisins
1½ tablespoons molasses
2 tablespoons cornstarch

Cook over low heat until mixture thickens and clears, stirring constantly. Spoon into 6 or more baked tart shells. Let cool slightly and serve while still warm. A scoop of ice cream is good on top.

Old-fashioned Cream Pie

Scald 1 pint milk. Beat together 1 egg, 1 cup sugar, 2 tablespoons flour, pinch of salt (¼ teaspoon); add slowly to the hot milk and thicken over fire. Flavor with vanilla or lemon. Pour into baked piecrust. Chill.

Children go for this — at least we surely did years ago. W.K.

Pecan Pie Anyone Can Make

Beat 3 eggs slightly; add
²⁄₃ cup sugar
1 cup white or dark corn syrup
¼ teaspoon salt
⅓ cup melted butter
¼ teaspoon vanilla

Mix thoroughly. Stir in 1 cup broken pieces of pecans. Pour in 9-inch pastry shell (unbaked). Bake in 375° oven 40-45 minutes or until set and pastry is nicely browned.

To test: Stick a silver knife, which has first been dipped in cold water, in center of pie. If knife comes out clean — pie is done.

Rhubarb Pie

3 cups fresh rhubarb, cut up
1 ¼ cups sugar
3 tablespoons flour
⅛ teaspoon salt
Pastry for 2-crust pie
2 tablespoons butter
¼ teaspoon nutmeg
1 teaspoon milk

Mix together first four ingredients. Fill pastry-lined pie pan. Dot with butter and sprinkle with nutmeg. Flute edges and prick top crust.

Bake at 425° for 15 minutes; then finish at 350° for 30 minutes.

Upside-down Peach Pie

1 well-buttered pie pan
Slice peaches in, rounding full
Cover with ⅓ cup sugar
Sprinkle with cinnamon
Dot with butter
Squeeze on juice of ½ lemon

Batter:

⅓ cup sugar
²⁄₃ tablespoon butter
Add pinch of salt and
1 well-beaten small egg
Sift ⅓ cup flour with ⅓ teaspoon baking powder, and add to batter, mixing well
Pour over peaches
Bake at 350° for 35-40 minutes

Eat warm — any topping might be good, ice cream, whipped cream, but it's extra-delicious straight.

Early cast-iron gypsy kettle with removable, portable folding handle. Like other pots with such handles, it was taken on journeys in covered wagons across the prairie. Such kettles were used for stews, soups, making soap, melting wax for candles, etc. It hung from a crane or trammel over the fireplace, or it could be set down upon the embers standing on its three short legs. Many strange legends and superstitions stem from such kettles which were sometimes called "witch pots" because of the magic potions old hags were supposed to have cooked in them. In Shakespeare's *Macbeth* such a pot is described as a cauldron in which the three witches are mixing a brew and chanting these famous lines: "Double, double, toil and trouble; fire burn and cauldron bubble." All through history such pots are portrayed as being connected with fire and brimstone, devils and demons, spooks and spirits, and the weirdest of witches. But out on the prairie it cooked many a delicious dinner over campfires for proud pioneers and spirited settlers who traveled the land.

Late nineteenth century skimmer and pierced ladle. The flatter piece is a skimmer, and the deeper one is the ladle. They are made of tinned sheet iron or tin plate.

125

Wrought iron eighteenth century down hearth toaster. Slices of bread were placed upright in the horizontal slots, and the toaster was set on the hearth before the fire. After the bread was toasted on one side, the piece was revolved on a center pivot pin so the other side of the bread could be toasted.

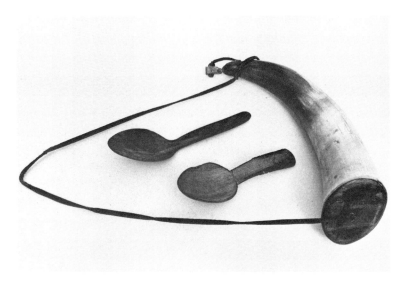

This old powder horn is like the one Pa Ingalls used when he went hunting. The spoons, also made of horn, were used for eating. Such items were hand-fashioned by pioneers and settlers. The tip of the powder horn has a little wooden plug that pulls out so that the horn could be filled with gunpowder.

This eighteenth century cast-iron tea kettle is bombe-shaped and has what is referred to as a gooseneck spout. It hung from a crane over the crackling fireplace. At one time it had three short feet on which it stood within the hearth, but due to long years of service over glowing embers, its little feet were worn down to nubbins.

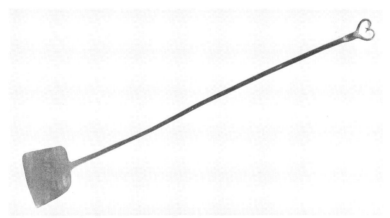

This wrought iron bread peel or "slice" dates from the eighteenth century and was used to slide loaves of bread in and out of the oven. Its long handle protected one from getting scorched, and it was especially made in such a length to insert bread well into the deep brick oven built in the wall next to the fireplace. Often the handle of such a piece was embellished with a bit of the blacksmith's art. Some handles were designed with ram's horn ends, while others (like the one pictured) were topped off with a little heart that no doubt was made for a loved one.

This old waffle iron was held by its long handle over the fire to bake waffles. One side is decorated with a heart. Back in the old days a young maiden served a fellow such a heart-decorated treat in hopes of having him fall in love with her, which adds up to the old saying, "The way to a man's heart is through his stomach."

Early eighteenth century cast-iron footed skillets. They stood in the fireplace over hot coals and cooked to perfection numerous tasty treats for the family to enjoy. Some were bowl-shaped, others had sides that flared out, and still others had round, flat bottoms with upright sides. Such cast-iron skillets have long, tapered handles often referred to in the past as "tails" because of their peculiar shapes.

13 PUDDINGS AND HARD SAUCE

Apple Pudding

5 or 6 apples
¾ cup flour
1 cup sugar
1 teaspoon baking powder
1 egg beaten
½ cup butter

Peel (not required), core the apples, and put in 1½-quart baking dish. Cover with ½ cup water. Mix and sift together flour, sugar, and baking powder. Add slightly beaten egg and pour (or crumble) over apples. Melt ½ cup butter and pour over all. Sprinkle lightly with cinnamon or nutmeg if desired. Cover. Bake at 350° for 45 minutes. Serve with a topping of whipped cream.

Apple pudding is so good in the fall, especially. Everyone should have an easy recipe so they can mix one up at the drop of a hat. W.K.

Jessie's Favorite Date Pudding

1 pound dates, chopped
¼ pound marshmallows, quartered
1 cup nuts, chopped
18 graham crackers rolled fine
10 tablespoons whole milk
1 teaspoon vanilla

Mix and form in roll; cover with waxed paper and chill in refrigerator.

Mrs. Truman's Ozark Pudding

1 egg
¾ cup sugar
2 tablespoons flour
1¼ teaspoons baking powder
Dash of salt
½ or 1 cup chopped apple
½ cup pecans

Beat egg well. Add sugar and beat until creamy. Sift flour, baking powder, and salt into egg mixture. Mix well. Add apple and pecans and mix. Pour into buttered 8-inch pie plate and bake in preheated 350° oven 35 minutes or until golden brown. Serve plain or with whipped cream or vanilla ice cream. (Serve hot, warm, or cold.) Makes 4 or 5 servings.

Do not be dismayed when this pudding rises high, then **falls** before time to remove it from the oven.

My Mother's Hard Sauce

Cream ½ cup of soft butter. Blend in gradually 1½ cups sifted confectioners' sugar and 2 teaspoons vanilla. If you like nutmeg, add ½ teaspoon to the sugar. Place in a cool spot to let it become hard as the name suggests.

Use on hot puddings. This is the dish little fingers were always dipping into on the sly.

Sarah Melander's Pineapple Pudding

1 large can crushed pineapple
Juice from pineapple
3 eggs, separated—reserve whites
1 cup sugar
1 tablespoon flour
Vanilla wafers
1 teaspoon vanilla and juice of 1 lemon

Combine in saucepan, pineapple juice, lemon juice, egg yolks, sugar, flour, and vanilla. Cook until thickened and set aside to cool. In deep, ovenproof dish, alternate layers of vanilla wafers, crushed pineapple, and sauce. Make a meringue of the three egg whites. Beat whites to soft-peak stage, then gradually add ½ cup sugar. Beat till stiff peaks are formed and sugar dissolved. Cover top of pudding and brown 12 to 15 minutes at 350°.

Thelma's Date Pudding

Dissolve:
　　1½ cups brown sugar in
　　1½ cups hot water in baking pan
Combine:
　　1 cup sugar
　　½ cup nuts
　　½ cup dates (chopped)
　　½ cup milk
　　1 cup flour
　　2 teaspoons baking powder
　　½ teaspoon salt
　　1 teaspoon vanilla

Mix together and drop into hot syrup and bake at 350° for 30 minutes.

Late nineteenth century cast-iron skillet with spouted sides for pouring off excess grease. Such pans were made well into the twentieth century, and their counterparts are still being bought and used today.

This late eighteenth century cast-iron herb or spice mill was also called a "ship-grinder" because of its boatlike shape, and a "sow and pig" mill because of a peculiar sound it made when in use. Herbs (or "yerbs" as some folks called them in the old days) or spices were put into the vessel-shaped part and the heavy wheel was rolled back and forth over them to crush or grind them. When the iron wheel scraped against the iron vessel, it caused an awful sound much like the squealing of pigs–thus its name, "sow and pig mill."

This nineteenth century tin biscuit oven stood on the hearth with its open side towards the fire. It baked delicious biscuits and Indian cakes made of cornmeal that were placed on the center shelf. The top has a convenient handle for carrying the piece away from the hearth, and the center shelf slides forward and lifts out for removing the biscuits after they were baked.

Early nineteenth century wrought iron dough scraper used when making bread dough in a dough box.

14 SALADS, SALAD DRESSINGS AND COTTAGE CHEESE

Aunt Nina's Waldorf Salad
Bea's Pea Salad
Boiled Salad Dressing
Cooked Salad Dressing
Mayonnaise Dressing
Homemade Cottage Cheese
Carolyn's Vegetable Molded Salad
Green Salad
Helen's Sweet-and-Sour Salad
Lime-Cottage Cheese Salad
Martha's Cottage Cheese Salad
My Shrimp Salad
Pauline's Perfection Salad
Sauerkraut Salad

Aunt Nina's Waldorf Salad

1 cup apples, chopped
1 cup celery, chopped
1 cup crushed pineapple, (drained)
1 cup nuts, chopped
1 cup marshmallows, chopped

Blend the above ingredients, mixing well. Make Lemon Sauce.

Lemon Sauce:

Juice of ½ lemon
1 cup sugar
1½ tablespoons flour
Small amount water
½ cup sweet cream

Combine ingredients in saucepan. Use a small amount of water, as you will want to make a thick sauce. When thickened, remove from heat and cool. Add ½ cup sweet cream to sauce and pour over other ingredients, mixing thoroughly. The lemon sauce makes the difference—also keeps the apples white. Try adding grapes—great.

Aunt Nina was a wonderful cook. She didn't need recipes for much of her cooking. She did it by heart and by hand. She always had a big garden and did lots of canning even after she was alone and didn't have anyone to cook for but herself. W.K.

Bea's Pea Salad

2 10-ounce packages of frozen peas
¼ cup chopped onions (red onions)
½ cup finely chopped celery
6 slices crisp bacon, crumbled
1 package slivered almonds
Sour cream to blend

Cook peas for about 4 minutes. (Do not let them get well done.) Drain if any water remains in pan and set aside to cool. When completely cool, mix peas with other ingredients and blend with sour cream. Toast the almonds for a few minutes and sprinkle on top before serving.

Serve on lettuce leaves. Serves 8 to 10. Super!

Boiled Salad Dressing

2 teaspoons sugar
1 teaspoon salt
1 teaspoon mustard
¾ cup water
1 egg, well beaten
2 tablespoons melted butter
¼ cup mild vinegar
Few grains cayenne
2 tablespoons flour

Combine dry ingredients. Add egg. Mix thoroughly. Cook over hot water, stirring constantly, until thick and smooth. Cool. Thin with whipped cream or evaporated milk before serving. If desired, more sugar may be added or honey may be substituted for sugar.

Cooked Salad Dressing

1 teaspoon dry mustard
1 to 2 tablespoons sugar
2 tablespoons flour
½ teaspoon salt
Dash of paprika
Mix in ½ cup cold water
In top of double boiler, beat:
1 whole egg or 2 yolks
¼ cup vinegar

Add the other mixed ingredients. Cook and stir over boiling water until thick and smooth. Add 2 tablespoons butter. It may be thinned with cream.

Mayonnaise Dressing

2 egg yolks
¼ cup vinegar
½ teaspoon dry mustard
½ teaspoon paprika
1 pint (2 cups) salad oil
1 teaspoon salt

Beat egg yolks and add a few drops of vinegar. Drop oil, drop by drop, into egg mixture until ¼ cup is used (beating all the time). Then gradually increase amount of oil added, beating constantly. As mixture thickens, add rest of vinegar a little at a time. Add salt, mustard, and paprika. Be sure to follow the directions.

Homemade Cottage Cheese

Pour milk into a wide bowl (country folks use raw milk). Set bowl aside in a warm place and let milk clabber or sour until it is thick. Then pour into a pan and heat very slowly over a very low flame until it separates from the water or whey. Stir occasionally. Put curds into a cloth bag like a flour sack or pillow slip and let hang from a clothesline until the liquid (whey) has drained out — or drain curds in a colander. Season with salt, pepper, and sweet cream for a richer tasting cheese. Any amount of raw or regular milk may be used, depending on how much cheese one wants to make.

Hmmm, this is really delicious. There's nothing like good homemade cottage cheese.

Carolyn's Vegetable Molded Salad

Dissolve 1 package lime gelatin in 1 cup hot water
Set aside to cool
Soften 1 package cream cheese (small size)
1 cup mayonnaise
½ cup canned milk
1 tablespoon chopped onion
2 tablespoons chopped green pepper
½ cup grated carrots
1 cup chopped celery
½ teaspoon salt

Blend together all ingredients. Pour cooled gelatin over mixture and stir together. Place in refrigerator to set.

Green Salad

1 package lime gelatin
No. 2½ can drained cut-up green-gage plums
Juice plus water to make 1¾ cups
Pinch salt
1 teaspoon lemon juice

Follow package instructions for gelatin. Refrigerate to congeal. Then add cut up plums. Refrigerate until firm. Whip together about 2 tablespoons mayonnaise and an 8-ounce package cream cheese; spread over gelatin and chill.

Try this with chicken, turkey, or ham.

Helen's Sweet-and-Sour Salad

2 (1-pound) cans sliced green beans
1 (1-pound) can garbanzo beans
1 can pimientos, diced
1 sweet red onion, sliced into thin rings
1 clove garlic
1 teaspoon salt
½ cup cider vinegar
⅔ cup sugar
½ cup salad oil
Pepper to taste

Drain and rinse beans. Combine with pimientos and onion slices. Crush garlic in salt. Combine with remaining ingredients in glass jar. Shake till well blended.

Pour over salad. Cover and marinate in refrigerator at least 24 hours. Serves 6.

Lime - Cottage Cheese Salad

Make lime gelatin according to directions. When partially set, add approximately 1 cup cottage cheese and the same amount of mayonnaise. Add drained crushed pineapple. Chill until firm.

A pretty, tasty, simple little salad.

Martha's Cottage Cheese Salad

Dissolve 1 package lemon gelatin in 1 cup hot tomato soup
When cool add:
1 cup cottage cheese
1 cup chopped green olives
1 cup chopped celery
1 cup chopped mango pepper
¼ teaspoon salt
2 tablespoons sugar
1 cup mayonnaise
Mix well and let stand in cool place until set firm.

My Shrimp Salad

Combine 3 cups cooked rice
2 cups cooked shrimp (deveined)
Toss with
¼ cup celery, diced
¼ cup chopped green pepper
¼ cup sliced stuffed olives
¼ cup pimiento
¼ cup minced onion
  Chill thoroughly. Salt and pepper to taste. Add 3 tablespoons mayonnaise.

Pauline's Perfection Salad

I level tablespoon Knox gelatin (unflavored)
¼ cup cold water
¼ cup mild vinegar
1 tablespoon lemon juice
1 cup boiling water
¼ cup sugar
½ teaspoon salt
½ cup cabbage, finely shredded
1 cup celery cut in small pieces
1 pimiento cut in small pieces (or green pepper)
  Soak gelatin in cold water 5 minutes. Add lemon juice, vinegar, boiling water, sugar, and salt. Refrigerate. When mixture begins to thicken, add remaining ingredients. Turn into mold and chill. Serve with Cooked Salad Dressing.
  I also add chopped green onions if available. This type salad should be used more often as it is so light and refreshing. W.K.

Sauerkraut Salad

Large size number 2 can kraut (do not drain)
1 large onion, chopped
1 bell pepper, chopped
1 cup celery, chopped
1 can red pimento, chopped
  Mix by tossing well. Add 1 cup sugar, cover. Refrigerate 24 hours. Mix well and serve.

This huge frying pan dates from the eighteenth century and is wrought from one piece of iron. In colonial inventories such pieces were often listed as "Ye Grete Fry Panns." They were passed down from one generation to the next and this one was found in an old slaves' quarters in Virginia. It measures nearly 43 inches in circumference, and indeed it is a "Grete Fry Pan."

This old iron griddle (sometimes called a girdle) hung from a crane over the fire and baked flat cakes or flap-jacks. The round ring on top of its half-loop handle was made to swivel so the piece could be turned in any direction. Such griddle cakes were turned with a spatula or turner.

An assortment of old spatulas and turners. The one with the wire loop is of japanned tin and dates from the late nineteenth century. The others are of wrought iron and date from the eighteenth century. The third example is decorated with a brass secret symbol to ward off evil, and the last example is extremely unusual, having a knop top with the initials "F.F." incised which acted as a seal. Often names and mystic emblems decorated the handles of the early types.

141

Front view

Back view

This early nineteenth century "tin kitchen" with its front and back views pictured, stood on the hearth with its open side facing the fire. It has a door that was lifted up to baste and look in on the meat or fowl it roasted. It stands on short legs and has handles at the top for carrying. Its open side, that stood before the flames, has a spit across the center that's held in place by each end resting in a hole on either side. One end of the spit is fitted with a handle that could be adjusted in a number of smaller holes on the side surrounding it to turn and position the food being cooked, like a turkey or a roast, so it could get done on all sides. The spit also has small, open slots into which skewers were impaled to keep meat or fowl in place. The drippings were caught in the deep, drumlike bottom of the roaster and poured out of a spout on the side so gravy could be made. Tin kitchens were made in various sizes and were also known as "reflector ovens" because at one time they were bright and shiny, and reflected the firelight. Some (like the one pictured) had doors that were decorated with hex marks to keep witches and devils from getting into the food and bewitching it. In the *Little House* book, a tin kitchen is illustrated roasting a prairie chicken.

15 WAYSIDE REMEDIES

Grandma Zenor's Remedy to Stop Bleeding
Grandma Zenor's Mustard Poultice

Grandma Zenor's Remedy to Stop Bleeding

Dissolve 1 level teaspoon of sugar in 3 ounces peroxide.
If in a hurry for a bad cut — cover with black pepper. Enough said. Secret, don't get cut. W.K.

Grandma Zenor's Mustard Poultice

2 tablespoons flour
1 tablespoon dry mustard
1 tablespoon water or enough to make a paste thin enough to spread on a piece of cloth large enough for the affected part of the body.

Spread the above over ½ of the cloth and fold the other half over it to cover it. Lay on affected part for 9 to 11 minutes. When skin looks red, take off. Wash with warm, soapy water. Dry and rub on a little olive oil or vaseline. Cover with soft white cloth.

Chances are you're going to feel better after this. Grandma Zenor had other remedies too, that could make one feel better and heal up quick. W.K.